10th Anniversary Edition

 BizBuySell

GUIDE TO SELLING YOUR BUSINESS

A roadmap to valuing your business and planning for a successful sale

BARBARA FINDLAY SCHENCK

In collaboration with BizBuySell

Limit of Liability/Disclaimer of Warranty: BizBuySell is a brand owned and operated by CoStar Realty Information, Inc. ("CoStar"). CoStar makes no representations or warranties with respect to the accuracy or completeness of the contents of this work and specifically disclaim all warranties, including without limitation warranties of merchantability, fitness for ordinary purposes or fitness for a particular purpose. No warranty may be created or extended by sales or promotional materials. The advice and strategies contained herein may not be suitable for every situation. CoStar is not engaged in rendering financial, legal, accounting, or other professional services and nothing in this work, including but not limited to, any materials or forms in the included Digital Toolkit, should be considered or used as such. If professional assistance related to the subject discussed in this work is required, the services of a competent professional person should be sought. COSTAR AND ITS AFFILIATES AND THEIR RESPECTIVE OFFICERS, DIRECTORS, EMPLOYEES AND THIRD-PARTY SUPPLIERS (COLLECTIVELY, THE "COSTAR PARTIES") WILL NOT BE HELD LIABLE FOR ANY DAMAGES SUFFERED OR INCURRED BY ANY CONSUMER OF THIS MATERIAL INCLUDING WITHOUT LIMITATION THOSE ARISING OUT OF OR RELATED TO ANY FAULTS, INACCURACIES, ERRORS OR OMISSIONS IN THE INFORMATION CONTAINED HEREIN. CoStar does not endorse the information or recommendations provided by an organization or website referred to in this work as a citation and/or a potential source of further information. Further, readers should be aware that internet websites listed in this work may have changed or disappeared between when this work was written and when it is read.

All rights reserved. No part of this book may be resold, reproduced, or transmitted in any form or by any means, electronic or mechanical, including photocopying, recording, or by any information storage and retrieval system without the prior written permission of CoStar.

BizBuySell
101 California Street, 43rd Fl.
San Francisco, CA 94111
www.BizBuySell.com

Copyright © 2023 CoStar Realty Information, Inc.
All rights reserved.
ISBN: 979-8-9879311-2-7

Library of Congress Control Number: 2023903862

Contents

Foreword	v
Introduction	vii
Part I: Valuing Your Business and Planning Your Exit	**1**
1. Estimating the Value of Your Business	**3**
The Asset Approach to Valuation	5
The Market Approach to Valuation	7
The Income Approach to Valuation	12
Circumstances That Alter the Business Valuation	13
The High Value of Business Sale Professionals	14
2. Defining What You Want Out of Your Business Sale	**21**
Defining Your Motivations and Objectives	22
Resolving Conflicts Between Your Exit Objectives and Your Desired Outcome	25
Understanding Your Sale Options	27
Setting Your Top Exit Priority	31
3. Planning Your Exit and Building Pre-Sale Business Value	**33**
Formulating Your Exit Strategy	34
Understanding What Business Buyers Want	37
Assessing Your Business as a Purchase Prospect	41
Identifying Pre-Sale Improvements to Attract Buyers and Build Value	42
Making Pre-Sale Decisions That Impact Sale Value and Taxes	50
Part II: Attracting Buyers and Selling Your Business	**55**
4. Launching the Sale of Your Business	**57**
Assembling Your Business Sale Team	58

Compiling Financial Records and Necessary Documents	64
Finalizing Your Asking Price	68
Preparing Your Business Selling Memorandum	71

5. Marketing Your Business for Sale — 77
Maintaining Confidentiality	78
Defining Your Likely Buyer	80
Creating Business-for-Sale Listings That Attract and Prequalify Buyers	83
Managing Your Listing and the Inquiries You Receive	90

6. Navigating the Selling Process — 95
Verifying Qualifications and Prioritizing Prospects for Follow-Up	96
Quickly Reaching and Beginning Discussions with Qualified Prospects	98
Preparing for Questions Buyers Are Likely to Ask	102
Determining Your Business Sale Payment Approach	109
Receiving and Accepting a Buyer/Seller Friendly Offer	114

7. Closing the Sale and Transferring the Business — 121
Performing Due Diligence	122
Structuring the Sale	128
Negotiating Final Terms and the Purchase and Sale Agreement	137
Understanding the Purchase and Sale Agreement	140
The Closing Process	142
Closing the Sale	144
Passing the Baton	147

Recommended Resources — 153
Index — 155

Foreword

Exiting a business is likely the biggest move a business owner will make. For most, it represents the conclusion of a career chapter that's provided a steady stream of income and, finally, the opportunity to reap the value built over years of hard work and creativity.

An established business with positive cash flow, skilled workers, competitive products and services, or even just a reputable brand has value for which other entrepreneurs would pay top dollar. But is your business ready to attract buyers? This guide helps you answer that question.

You'll discover how planning is critical to receiving the full value for what you've worked so hard to build, while passivity and procrastination can be costly. Whether you're looking to sell immediately, or in the near or more-distant future, now is the time to chart your roadmap to a sale that allows you to exit on your own terms.

As the Internet's leading business-for-sale marketplace, we are pleased to provide this informative guide authored by Barbara Findlay Schenck, now in its fully updated 10th Anniversary edition. This guide will enrich you with knowledge to apply during presale preparation, working with industry experts, navigating the sale process, and help you successfully pass the business on to a new owner.

Introduction

Since its first publication, BizBuySell's *Guide to Selling Your Small Business* has led countless owners through the exit process, helping them to harvest the final round of value before turning their businesses over to new owners. Its actionable advice and step-by-step instructions have become a widely recognized roadmap through the sale process, from first defining motivations and objectives to preparing the business for sale, launching a plan for reaching qualified buyers, negotiating a purchase offer, and, finally, completing a sale that allows owners to exit on their own terms and conditions.

This 10th Anniversary edition of the *Guide to Selling Your Business* updates and optimizes the roadmap, helping you plan your exit and sell when ready. It addresses the questions on the minds of business owners in today's business-for-sale marketplace, beginning with the primary methods of business valuation before detailing long- and short-term strategies for enhancing and protecting value. It then leads you through the entire business sale process, which typically takes 6-12 months. Through each step, it provides valuable advice and helps you maintain confidentiality as you aim to reach and negotiate with buyers and achieve a sale that meets your financial goals.

Plus, this new and enhanced edition features an all-new set of digital forms and worksheets to help you customize your own personal roadmap and prepare for a successful business exit. You can access this downloadable digital toolkit at no cost by visiting https://www.bizbuysell.com/seller/guide/selling-a-business/.

When you own a business, the question isn't whether you will someday leave its ownership behind, but rather when that exit will take place and how you will reap final value from the business you have built. Count on this guide to deliver advice and steps to follow on the exit path ahead.

Guide Objectives

- A detailed explanation of business valuation, exit planning, and the selling process.
- Ways to enhance the value of your business and prepare it for sale.
- Advice on how to price, present, and market your business for sale.
- Best practices for assembling your team of business sale advisors, communicating with prospective buyers, navigating the sale process, and maintaining confidentiality.
- Details on ways to structure the sale, negotiate the deal, and pass the ownership and success of the business you have built to a new owner.
- Resources on professionals to rely on through the entire process.

Using This Guide

The seven chapters of this guide are presented in two parts:

Part I: These three chapters outline the steps for creating a plan for protecting your future and exiting your business when the time is right. They help you determine the current value of your business, assess whether your business is a strong sale prospect, and undertake pre-sale improvements that enhance sale attractiveness and value. Count on this part to provide step-by-step information for creating a sound exit plan to follow.

Part II: These four chapters present essential steps to follow from the moment you decide to sell to the moment you pass the keys to a new owner. They guide you through the process of preparing and pricing your business for sale and selecting your team of sale advisors before listing and marketing your business for sale; finding, screening, and negotiating with buyers; navigating the sale transaction; and, finally, closing the sale and transferring business ownership.

Additional Valuable Resources

Professional Business Brokers: First and foremost, we want you to achieve success. In addition to the information in this guide, a professional business broker can offer a wealth of expert advice and assistance on business valuation, exit planning, assessing business sale-readiness, business pricing, finding buyers and conducting buyer negotiations. To locate a broker, visit the BizBuySell Broker Directory.

BizBuySell: For over 25 years, BizBuySell has been the Internet's leading business-for-sale marketplace where hundreds of thousands of businesses have been bought and sold. BizBuySell has a large inventory of businesses listed for sale, a leading franchise directory, and one of the largest databases of for-sale and sold business comparables. The BizBuySell website also features tools, advice and resources for business buyers and sellers. *To stay on top of the latest news and information on the process of selling a business, go to https://www.bizbuysell.com and click "join" for a free BizBuySell membership.* On Facebook, follow @bizbuysell. On Instagram, follow @officialbizbuysell, On Twitter, follow @BizBuySell.

This guide is produced by BizBuySell and written by Barbara Findlay Schenck, who with her husband, Peter, started, grew, and sold an advertising agency before becoming a columnist and presenter on how to plan, market, brand and sell a business. She is the author or coauthor of best-selling books including *Small Business Marketing for Dummies, Business Plans Kit for Dummies,* and *Branding for Dummies.*

Part I
Valuing Your Business and Planning Your Exit

1

Estimating the Value of Your Business

You may be ready to sell and exit your business now, or you may be planning to grow it for a few more years before offering it for sale. Either way, understanding its current sale value is the first step in planning and protecting your future.

In the same way that a medical checkup assesses your current physical condition and provides information that guides your healthcare decisions, a business valuation assesses the current condition and value of your business and provides information that guides your business planning, exit planning, planning for pre-sale improvements, and sale timing decisions.

By estimating the value of your business — creating at least a back-of-the-envelope estimated price — you will have the information you need to determine whether your business today meets the financial objectives you are aiming for in a sale and, if not, to determine the extent of improvements required and the amount of time necessary to achieve them.

Three widely accepted valuation approaches lead to an estimate of business value, which almost always is revised, with professional assistance, prior to finalizing the sale asking price.

- **The asset approach** estimates the fair market value of the physical assets of a business that could be converted to cash. This assessment is especially important to owners of distressed businesses who are likely to liquidate tangible assets. It is also important when substantiating the price of the business during sale negotiations and due diligence.
- **The market approach** projects estimated value of a business based on sale prices of comparable businesses. It involves accessing and analyzing data from recent transactions and dividing sale prices by business revenues or earnings to arrive at the multiple at which the sales of comparable businesses have closed.
- **The income approach** estimates the value of future business cash flows or income. It is especially important when valuing startups or turnarounds for which past financial performance is not a good indicator of future potential. The approach involves either a capitalization of earnings method or a discounted cash flow method to project growth, with both benefitting from professional valuation and accounting advice.

No one valuation approach answers the question, "What's my business worth?" Instead, a combination of approaches contributes to the answer based on the value of your business assets, sale prices of comparable businesses, and the annual earnings and strength of your business as a going concern.

This chapter provides you with valuation information you can use on your own and as you call on assistance from professionals. It guides you through the following:
- The business valuation approaches.

- How to calculate seller's discretionary earnings (SDE), a key figure in pricing calculations.
- The earnings multiple that applies in most valuation estimates of businesses like yours.
- When to call on outside professionals and business brokers for assistance.

Step 1: The Asset Approach to Valuation

This approach establishes the fair market or sale value of the tangible, physical assets of your business.

- **The asset valuation includes** all physical assets of the business including fixtures, furnishings, equipment, inventory, real estate, and other physical assets
- **The asset valuation does not include** the value of intangible assets such as brand recognition and reputation, websites and online presence, client lists and relations, skilled workforce, trademarks, patents and trade secrets, and intellectual property that will transfer to a new owner. Intangible assets are included when assessing goodwill value and almost always require assistance from professional valuation experts.

A valuation of assets is essential throughout the sale process:

- *During exit planning*, the asset valuation provides a sense of the total value of all physical assets that could be converted to cash. If, after completing a business valuation, the sale value of physical assets is very similar to the price likely to be received through a business sale, liquidation — simply selling assets and closing shop — becomes the most expedient exit route. Liquidation also becomes the necessary exit route for owners of businesses that are not in condition to attract a buyer at the time the owner wants or needs to make an immediate exit, a condition Chapter 3 of this guide aims to help your business avoid.

- *During business sale negotiations*, the asset valuation substantiates a component of the business pricing strategy. It presents an asset inventory and a sound projection of what it would cost the buyer to otherwise purchase the furnishings, fixtures, equipment, and other physical assets of your business, in their current condition and at their current market value.
- *During the due diligence phase of a business sale*, the asset valuation confirms all assets being transferred and whether each asset is owned outright or financed, and whether specific assets are accompanied by service agreements or other obligations.

Conducting an Asset Valuation

Begin by listing all physical assets of your business. Make an inventory by going room by room, department by department, or location by location. Or group assets by type, such as office furniture, office equipment, production equipment, office furnishings, leasehold improvements, automobiles, and so on, also noting the location of each asset.

For each asset, record the date of acquisition, original cost, replacement cost, and current fair market value, which is the sale value of the asset in its current condition.

Use the **Asset Valuation Worksheet in the Digital Toolkit** as you create and value your asset inventory. The form automatically calculates column entries. It also includes a column for notes regarding ownership, such as the amount of the purchase price outstanding, the cost of accompanying service agreements, and other costs of ownership. Access the digital toolkit by visiting https://www.bizbuysell.com/seller/guide/selling-a-business/.

Be aware that the resulting asset valuation will differ from the asset value shown on your business balance sheet for two reasons:

1. The balance sheet reflects the book value or carrying value of assets based on acquisition cost minus depreciation, while the asset valuation reflects the fair market value of assets which, in some cases, could be even more than their initial price.

2. The balance sheet reflects the depreciated value only of assets acquired at prices above a minimum value, while the asset valuation includes the market value of all physical assets minus any liabilities associated with those assets.

Also be aware that there are situations that may require asset valuations by an independent certified appraiser. For example, if production equipment assets are being used as collateral for a bank loan, the valuation will require assessment by an independent certified machinery appraiser. Likewise, other high-value assets may require fair and impartial appraisals that can hold up under scrutiny with courts, banks, and financial institutions.

> **Step 1: Key Takeaways**
>
> The asset approach establishes the value of the tangible or physical assets of a business:
>
> - An asset valuation allows owners with immediate exit priorities to weigh the value of liquidation versus business sale.
> - An asset valuation substantiates a component of business pricing during due diligence and price negotiations.
> - Valuation of high-value assets may require fair and impartial professional appraisals.

Step 2: The Market Approach to Valuation

The market approach estimates the value of your business based on data from similarly sized and recently sold businesses in your geographic area or business sector. It involves multiplying the earnings of your business by the valuation multiple at which similar businesses have sold or are selling.

Accessing Comparable Data

Often referred to as comps, comparable data is usually sourced through online databases tracking recent listed and recently sold businesses. These databases are typically accessed through business brokers or professional appraisers. You can also access comparable data by visiting BizBuySell.com.

Comp criteria can be targeted by industry, geographic location, financial performance, sale price, and other filters. This allows a comparison of information only from businesses that are similar to yours in terms of industry classification, geographical location, size (revenue, assets, employees), earnings, and other financial metrics.

Using Comparable Data to Establish Valuation Benchmarks

Knowledge of the price-to-revenues or price-to-earnings ratios at which businesses similar to yours have recently closed provides a benchmark for the valuation multipliers you might use to arrive at a ballpark estimate of your business value.

The goal is to compare businesses like yours in terms of industry classification, geographical location, size (in terms of revenue, assets, employees), earnings, and other financial metrics.

For example, the owner of a California pizzeria could compile a BizBuySell Valuation Report for comparable pizzerias sold in California. Based on the report results, the owner could divide the sale price of each recently sold pizzeria by its gross revenue or earnings to see the range of pricing multiples at which comparable businesses have recently sold.

The owner would then study the report data in search of information reflecting the condition of each business, based on such indicators as expenses, rent, or other data. Considering how the condition of recently sold pizzerias compare with the condition of the owner's pizzeria would help determine if it ranks in the higher – or the lower – quartile of businesses in terms of condition, and therefore whether its valuation would be based on the higher – or lower – multiples achieved through recent sales.

Understanding the Difference Between Price-to-Revenues and Price-to-Earnings Ratios

When reviewing data for comparable market sales, two of the most common ratios used are revenue multiples (often referred to as sales multiples) and earnings multiples.

- **Revenue multiples** are based on the gross revenue shown on the annual business income statement. They involve a fixed figure, and therefore some experts feel applying a multiple to annual gross revenue is the most reliable approach. However, because annual revenues cannot reflect how much money the business actually earns, most experts caution that basing the price multiple on revenues does not reflect the health of the business. Revenues do not reflect whether the business is mismanaged or if it has higher-than-average expenses.
- **Earnings multiples** are based on how much the business earns annually for the benefit of its owner. Owner earnings differ from the annual profit shown on the business year-end income statement or its federal tax return. When pricing small businesses, profit and earnings are defined as follows:

Profit, the bottom line on the business income statement, reflects all business revenue less all legally deductible business expenses to arrive at the lowest possible taxable income.

Annual owner earnings, also called *owner's cash flow or seller's discretionary earnings (SDE),* also include all business revenue, but from there deductions reflected on the income statement are revised to arrive at a total showing how much the business actually generates for the benefit of its owner in a normal year.

Preparing a Statement of Seller's Discretionary Earnings (SDE)

To calculate SDE, a key figure in small business sales, the year-end income statement is recast with the following adjustments:

1. Add back expenses that were deducted for interest, depreciation, taxes, and amortization, resulting in what accountants call business EBIDTA (earnings before interest depreciation, taxes, and amortization).
2. Add back expenses that benefitted the owner directly, such as owner's salary and benefits, insurance, and auto use.
3. Add back discretionary expenses and contributions or

donations that another owner might choose not to incur.
4. Add back non-recurring expenses to "normalize" earnings by excluding unusual and one-time transactions of the business
5. If SDE has differed greatly over recent years, work with your accountant to create and present what is called a weighted average.
6. To prepare an estimate of your SDE, use the **SDE Calculation Worksheet in the Digital Toolkit**, working from your financial statements to fill in the shaded cells. The form automatically calculates entries to reflect your annual owner's benefit – your seller's discretionary earnings or SDE – which forms the basis of the income-based valuation used in pricing nearly all small and medium-sized businesses.

Calculating the Earnings Multiple

The earnings multiple used in most small business valuations is a number between 1 and 5. Businesses with weakest potential and highest risk have the lowest multiples, and businesses with strongest potential and lowest risk have the highest multiples.

When applied to the SDE of the business, the multiple results in an early estimate of business value. For example, a business with SDE of $500,000 and a multiple of 3 has an estimated value of $1,500,000, while a business with SDE of $500,000 and a multiple of 4 has an estimated value of $2,000,000.

To determine the multiple for your business, begin by studying comparable-data benchmarks, described in the previous section. They provide the most basic ballpark estimates of earnings multiples for businesses matching your size, geographic location, or business sector.

You can begin to estimate the earnings multiple for your business by assessing factors likely to signal attractiveness or risk to buyers.

To begin, open the **Earnings Multiple Assessment Worksheet in the Digital Toolkit**. It lists the major risk factors, including annual earnings, revenues and profits, financial records, clientele, products, recurring revenue, staffing, location, brand and reputation, and more.

1: Estimating the Value of Your Business

Consider the questions that accompany each factor and assign a number from 1 to 5 that you feel accurately reflects the condition of your business, with 1 indicating the weakest condition and 5 the strongest condition. The form automatically averages ratings to provide an early sense of the earnings multiple that your business, in its current condition and based on your assessment, might command.

CAUTION: Be aware that the multiple you arrive at is based on your assessment at this time. The result will almost certainly be adjusted prior to pricing, based on expert input from your sale advisers, the condition of your business at the time of sale offering, sale terms, and other conditions that affect attractiveness to buyers.

Doing the Math

This is the easy part of estimating value using the market approach.

- You have analyzed comparable sales data and learned the multiples achieved by recent sales of businesses similar to yours.
- Based on market comps and your own assessment of the condition of your business, you have estimated the multiple to use when roughly estimating your business value.
- You have recast your year-end income statement to arrive at your seller's discretionary earnings (SDE).

You are now a simple calculation away from creating a ballpark estimate of the value of your business:

SDE x Earnings Multiple = Estimated Business Value

That single calculation results in the estimated value of your business.

CAUTION: Take the word "estimated" seriously for a number of reasons:

- Business valuators agree that the business owner may not be the best person to assess the strength and attractiveness of the business and therefore its earnings multiple.
- Even after a business valuation is established, it is subject to change due to changes in business conditions.
- Business sale prices typically include fixtures, furnishings, and

equipment, normal inventory, and intangible assets, but not owned real estate, which is valued separately.

Valuation involves layers of complexity. Involve business advisors and your broker to provide valuable assistance in making the assessments that contribute to the earnings multiple calculation.

> **Step 2: Key Takeaways**
>
> The market approach begins with an analysis of data from recent sales of similar businesses:
>
> - Most business valuations involve a multiple of business revenues or earnings.
> - Data from comparable business sales provides a benchmark for determining the multiple used in the business valuation formula, with the benchmark adjusted to reflect business conditions, strengths, and risks.
> - Most business valuations apply a 1 to 5 multiple not to business revenues or profits, but to annual seller's discretionary earnings (SDE), a recast version of the income statement that reflects how much the business actually generates annually for the benefit of the owner.
> - SDE x Earnings Multiple = Estimated Business Value
> - Take the word "estimated" seriously. Until the time of a sale offering, business valuation will be adjusted based on professional input, changes in business conditions, sales terms, and buyer negotiations.

Step 3: The Income Approach to Valuation

The income approach values a business based upon its expected future performance and cash flows, which are calculated by projecting current business earnings and then adjusting for changes in anticipated future growth rates, cost structure, and other factors that affect earnings.

The income valuation is based on either capitalization of earnings or discounted cash flow:

- **Capitalization of earnings** measures the value of a business by determining the net present value (NPV) of expected future profits or cash flows. This involves dividing the expected future earnings of the business by the capitalization rate, which is the rate of return the buyer can expect to earn on the investment made to purchase the business. The capitalization rate is determined in part by the company's perceived risks. This method is often used by businesses with stronger future growth and profit projections than past performance indicates.
- **Discounted cash flow (DCF)** estimates the value of a business based on its projected future earnings. First, the expected cash flow of the business is projected over a duration of time, usually one year. That projection is then discounted based on risk, using a percentage which is either derived from weighted average cost of capital (WACC) or a build-up rate determined by the market.

All valuation approaches, and especially the income approach, benefit from the knowledge and expertise of experienced professionals, listed in the upcoming Step 5 titled "The High Value of Business Sale Professionals."

Step 4: Circumstances That Alter the Business Valuation

Until the time of a sale offering, business valuation will be adjusted to account for changing conditions, including:
- Changes affecting your business sector and market area may affect the value of your business and the price a buyer might be willing to pay for it.
- Changes altering economic conditions may affect your sales volume and profit margins, also affecting the annual earnings upon which multiple-of-earning valuations are based.
- Departure of key personnel or major clients, or other major

business changes, may affect business value and attractiveness.

Beyond adjustments due to circumstances, prior to a sale listing the asking price will be further adjusted based on the following circumstances:

- If the sale offering includes seller financing – the seller's willingness to accept a portion of the purchase price in payments that are not due until a defined point in the future – the attractiveness of the sale offering increases. Some studies show that by offering seller financing, the earnings multiple used in the price calculation can increase by as much as a third, resulting in higher business value.
- Because business buyers negotiate downward from the business asking price, sale pricing is often set at 10-15 percent over valuation to account for the effect of buyer negotiation. Of the thousands of closed business sale transactions reported to BizBuySell each year, most sales closed at approximately ninety percent of the asking price.

> **Step 4: Key Takeaways**
>
> Valuation estimates are adjusted prior to sale pricing to account for:
> - Changes in the business sector.
> - Changes in economic conditions.
> - Changes in business staffing or clientele.
> - The owner's decision regarding whether to provide seller financing.
> - Anticipated buyer price negotiations.

Step 5: The High Value of Business Sale Professionals

The surest way to arrive at a valuation for your business is to follow the guidance on the preceding pages and to seek guidance from professionals experienced in business assessments, valuations, and sales.

When and Where to Seek Guidance

- Seek guidance from a business appraiser or valuation expert if your business owns intellectual property or involves proprietary processes, a valuable brand, or other assets that are unique and therefore difficult to value and price.
- Seek guidance from business consultants if your selling price could be significantly higher following major business improvements that are beyond the expertise of you and your management team.
- Seek guidance from a broker if you need help placing a value and price on your business, maintaining confidentiality about your sale, finding and dealing with prospective buyers, and taking on the demands of selling your business – while you keep running it efficiently.
- Seek guidance from a merger and acquisition (M&A) specialist or from an attorney with M&A expertise if your business has annual sales over $5 million or annual SDE over $1 million, as it is likely to attract another business as its buyer, and the sale will be complex.
- Seek guidance from a local Small Business Development Center (SBDC) for help with business planning, financial management, and much more. America's SBDC is a nationwide network, funded in part through the U.S. Congress and Small Business Administration, that offers a wide range of free and low-cost services to small businesses.

Choosing a Broker

Business brokers offer in-depth insights on valuation, marketing, prospecting, negotiations, and other fundamental sale elements. Most have extensive prior business experience that allows them to understand the financial, operational, and legal aspects of a business.

From sale preparation through the sale process, their role is to streamline the process, focusing on the deal while the owner focuses on maintaining business operations and strengths.

Most broker's charge a percentage of the sale as their fee. In return they provide a number of benefits:

- Experience in the business sale arena and process.
- Knowledge of comparable business sale values.
- Ability to professionally present the business and attract prospective buyers through extended networks and listings on heavily trafficked sites.
- Access to a database of prospective qualified buyers.
- Ability to establish confidential contact with targeted prospective buyers.
- Experience assisting with business preparation, valuation, and sale materials, although sometimes at an additional fee.
- Guidance and expertise through the buyer negotiations, due diligence, financing, closing documents, and the final business transition from seller to buyer.
- Experience in business sales and familiarity with most challenges that can arise.

Brokers are especially valuable for business owners who are uncertain about valuation, who are unclear about how or where to find prospective buyers, who lack time to run the business while also planning for and negotiating a sale, and who have little expertise in marketing, presenting, and negotiation.

When seeking a qualified broker, check out the BizBuySell Broker Directory, the largest online broker directory, which includes thousands of professionals who can assist with business sales.

You can also contact the International Business Brokers Association (IBBA) at https://www.ibba.org.

When it's time to interview brokers, the **Business Broker Questionnaire in the Digital Toolkit** provides questions to ask.

Following this deep dive into business valuation, you now have the basis for estimating the value of your business today, in its current condition, and knowing the resources to call on for help. You are now ready to begin seriously thinking about your exit plan, the topic of Chapter 2.

> **Step 5: Key Takeaways**
>
> Rely on professionals experienced in business assessments, valuations, and sales:
> - *Rely on business appraisers and valuation experts* when valuing intellectual property.
> - *Rely on business consultants* when planning value-enhancing business improvements.
> - *Rely on business brokers* for business valuation and pricing, finding and dealing with buyer prospects, and handling the demands of a business sale while you keep running the business efficiently.
> - *Rely on merger and acquisition (M&A) specialists* if your business is likely to attract another business as its buyer, if its sale value and future potential is high, and if the sale will be complex.

Key Terms

Asset Valuation: An estimate of the fair market value of all tangible assets owned by a business that could be converted to cash, including such physical items as furnishings, fixtures, equipment, inventory, and real estate but excluding intangible business assets such as brand recognition and reputation, websites and online presence, client lists and client relations, talented workforce, and other intangible elements, which together are valued separately, often with professional valuation assistance, and included in the goodwill value of the business.

Market Valuation: An estimate of business value based on data, referred to as comps, from recent listings or sales of similarly sized businesses in the same geographic location and/or business sector to determine the multiple of revenues or earnings at which comparable businesses are being offered or sold.

Earnings Multiple: A number, usually between 1 and 5 but sometimes higher for large or very profitable businesses, that reflects the profitability, future strength, and attractiveness of a business and that is used, when multiplied by seller's discretionary earnings, to roughly estimate sale value.

Going Concern Value: The value of all the assets of a business plus its worth as an ongoing entity, based on its recent past performance attracting and retaining customers and experiencing financial success.

Goodwill: The value of intangible assets of a business, including brand recognition and reputation, websites and online presence, client lists and client relations, talented workforce, industry and community standing, and other positive elements that contribute to business strength.

Income Valuation: An estimate of the value of a business based on future business cash flows or income. It is most used when valuing startups or turnarounds for which past financial performance is not a good indicator of future potential. The approach involves either a capitalization-of-earnings method or a discounted-cash-flow method to project growth, both of which rely on professional valuation and accounting advice.

Intellectual Property: Trademarks, patents, and trade secrets which almost always require valuation assistance from professional valuation experts.

Liquidation: Ending a business by selling its physical assets with no compensation for the intangible assets of the business. An asset-based valuation shows what is considered the liquidation or "floor value" of the business.

Seller Financing: A sale payment approach that allows the business buyer to pay a portion of the purchase price when the sale closes, and to pay the remainder of the price, plus interest, over a specified period, usually backed by security and other agreements.

Seller's Discretionary Earnings (SDE): The amount a business generates annually for the benefit of its owner and a key figure of interest to business buyers. SDE differs from business profit by adding back deductions for owner salary, insurance, auto use, memberships, and other benefits; discretionary expenses another owner may choose

1: Estimating the Value of Your Business

not to make; expenses for non-recurring purchases; and deductions for interest, taxes, depreciation, and amortization. Also called annual earnings or owner's cash flow.

Digital Toolkit Resources

Access the digital toolkit by visiting https://www.bizbuysell.com/seller/guide/selling-a-business/.

Asset Valuation Worksheet
SDE Calculation Worksheet
Earnings Multiple Assessment Worksheet
Business Broker Questionnaire

2

Defining What You Want Out of Your Business Sale

Chapter 1 was all about setting your exit starting point by finding the answer to your first question: What's my business worth? It helped you arrive at the estimated value of your business in its current condition.

Chapter 2 is all about developing your plan for going forward. If you could ask a GPS app to map the route from today to your business exit, you'd see three options. The longest route would be the one that includes making value-enhancing business improvements prior to a sale listing.

The midrange route would involve offering the business for sale in its current condition. The shortest route would be liquidation by selling not the business but rather only its tangible assets, often at bargain prices.

As you select the exit route you'll follow, this chapter guides you through the major considerations involved:

- Defining and prioritizing your exit motivations, timeframe and objectives.
- Understanding the most common exit options and what's

involved with each.
- Matching your financial and timing priorities with exit options.
- Selecting an exit approach that achieves your financial objectives, sale-approach objectives and after-sale objectives.

Reading this chapter will take minutes, but making the decisions involved requires a worthwhile investment of time and thought. Worksheets in the Digital Toolkit will help as you set the exit plan you'll follow.

Step 1: Defining Your Motivations and Objectives

Before you can zero in on your preferred exit approach, you need to do some pre-exit self-reflection.

- What circumstances are driving your desire or need to exit, and how urgent or flexible is your exit timeframe?
- What do you want to achieve financially from your business sale?
- Post-sale, do you want to exit immediately, do you want to remain involved with the business only during the ownership transition, or do you want to stay involved for a longer period?
- Post-sale, do you have preferences for how the business will continue under new ownership?

The next sections help as you consider your answers to these questions and decide which sale approach best aligns with your objectives.

Defining Your Exit Planning Circumstances and Urgency

Owner exits are usually prompted by one or several circumstances, with no one reason applying to all or even most exits. Use the **Motivations and Timing Worksheet in your Digital Toolkit**, which you can access by visiting https://www.bizbuysell.com/seller/guide/selling-a-business/. Then, consider whether any of the following are motivating your decision making:

1. Do you want to retire?

2: Defining What You Want Out of Your Business Sale

2. Are you bored by your business?
3. Are you feeling burned out?
4. Are there business challenges that require time and financial investment beyond what you can or want to provide?
5. Is there a desire or need to relocate to a different geographic region?
6. Is divorce, a family issue, or other personal challenges prompting you to sell?
7. Are financial pressures, including the need to free up money or to make more money than the business can provide, an issue behind your exit motivation?
8. Are you facing health challenges?
9. Is there a new opportunity you'd like to pursue?
10. Are you facing partner conflicts or other internal business issues?

After listing which circumstances are motivating your exit decision, note whether your exit timing is urgent or flexible. Realize that the most urgent exit needs often correlate with lower sale prices for three main reasons:

- Immediate exits eliminate the opportunity to strengthen business performance and attractiveness prior to a sale listing.
- Immediate exits prompted by pressing financial needs almost always force an immediate sale and payoff, precluding the opportunity to offer seller financing, which typically supports a higher sale price.
- Immediate exits shorten or eliminate the possibility of seller involvement in a post-sale transition period, which likely leads to concerns that can lower a buyer's offer.

Defining Your Financial Priorities

Beyond personal circumstances, exit decisions involve financial priorities, which are affected by timing realities:

- **Do you want to achieve the highest-possible sale price, or is timing more important than pricing?** Consider that unless a

business is in a strong financial and operational condition, an immediate sale likely results in a discounted price.
- **Do you want or need a full payout or a significant payment at sale closing?** Consider that most cash payoffs require buyers to seek third-party loans, which are often hard to come by and slow to process. They also often result in lower selling prices.

Defining Your Post-Sale Considerations

Understanding what you want to do after a sale also influences your sale-approach decision:

- **Do you want to exit and immediately walk away from the business?** Consider that unless the business is in strong condition and easy to transition to a new owner, the seller's desire for a rapid departure raises doubts and leads to a lower selling price, especially if the seller also seeks an all-cash payoff.
- **Are you willing to remain involved during a 3- to 12-month transition period?** Consider that a seller's willingness to remain with the business for a post-sale period conveys to buyers higher confidence in the future of the business, which in turn supports a higher selling price.
- **After the sale, do you want to remain involved, full- or part-time, as a partner, consultant, or employee?** Consider that in many cases, the seller's desire for ongoing involvement limits the buyer pool and triggers price negotiations.

As part of post-sale considerations, also list what you want for your business, clients, and staff:

- **Is it important to you that your business remain at its current location with only limited disruption to clients and staff?** Consider that a desire to keep the business in its current location and configuration reduces the option of a merger or consolidation with another business, narrows the buyer pool, and usually affects pricing.

2: Defining What You Want Out of Your Business Sale

> **Step 1: Key Takeaways**
>
> Planning your business exit begins by defining your motivations and objectives:
> - The circumstances driving your desire or need to exit.
> - The urgency or flexibility of your exit timeframe.
> - Your financial hopes or expectations.
> - Your desire to exit immediately or to remain with the business post-sale, either during the transition period or for a longer period.
> - Your conditions, if any, for how and where the business will continue under new ownership.

Step 2: Resolving Conflicts Between Your Exit Objectives and Your Desired Outcome

Various exit objectives conflict with one another. Before finalizing the list of what you want out of your exit, use the following list to reconsider and prioritize your motivations.

Desire for the highest possible price *conflicts with* **desire for all-cash payoff, immediate departure, post-sale involvement, or post-sale priorities.**

Why? First, sales requiring all-cash payoffs typically close at considerably lower prices than those involving seller financing. Second, sellers requiring an immediate departure signal to the buyer a high sale desire, which invites price negotiations. Finally, stipulating post-sale priorities for the owner or the business often narrows the buyer pool and decreases the ability to sell for the highest possible price.

Desire for all-cash at closing *conflicts with* **desire for immediate sale, a high price, or immediate departure.**

Why? All-cash payoffs often require difficult-to-obtain and slow-to-process third-party loans. They also signal urgent seller motivation, which can lead to lower sale prices.

Desire for immediate sale *conflicts with* **desire for a high price and desire for immediate departure.**

Why? Almost all businesses require a period of time for pre-sale preparation to enhance business attractiveness, strength and value. And almost all businesses that appear less attractive and valuable are slower to attract buyer interest.

Desire for immediate departure *conflicts with* **desire for a high price or all-cash payoff.**

Why? Unless the business is in strong condition and very easy to transition to a new owner, rapid departure raises buyer doubts and leads to lower pricing. To a business buyer, a request for immediate departure, like a request for an all-cash payoff, is an indication of either the seller's high desire to sell or low confidence in the future of the business, both resulting in lower purchase offers.

Desire for post-sale personal or business priorities *conflicts with* **desire for a high price.**

Why? Stipulating future personal involvement or after-sale priorities for the business limits the buyer pool and triggers price negotiations.

Desire for a pre-sale business preparation period followed by a strong sale offering *conflicts with* **no other sale objective.**

Why? With a mid-term to long-term time frame, the seller can improve the condition, attractiveness, and value of the business while planning a sale offering that addresses seller objectives and avoids conflicting priorities.

As you consider your exit objectives, two worksheets in the Digital Toolkit can help. The one titled **Prioritizing Sale Objectives** helps you gauge on a scale of 1-10 how important each sale outcome is to you. The **Conflicting Objectives Worksheet** summarizes how desired outcomes can preclude one another and can help as you reassess which objectives are your highest sale priorities.

2: Defining What You Want Out of Your Business Sale

> **Step 2: Key Takeaways**
>
> Personal exit motivations guide your exit and sale decisions:
> - Desire for immediate sale often conflicts with desire for the highest price or all-cash payoff.
> - Desire for the highest possible price often conflicts with desire for all-cash payoff at closing, immediate departure, post-sale involvement, or other post-sale priorities.
> - Desire for all-cash payoff at closing often precludes immediate sale, a high price, or immediate departure.
> - Desire for post-sale involvement or post-sale priorities often precludes a high price.
> - Desire for a mid-term to longer-term pre-sale planning period during which business improvements enhance business value prior to a sale offering precludes no other sale objectives.

Step 3: Understanding Your Sale Options

Whether you're selling only the physical assets of your business, selling a portion of your business, or selling the entirety of your business, when you're ready to exit, you have options, and each option has issues that need to be considered.

Option 1. Selling Your Part of the Business to an Existing Partner

Most partnerships are launched with legal documents that include a buy-sell agreement. If a partnership agreement is in place (and you should never enter a partnership without one), it stipulates the pre-defined route for a partner exit – including the price and procedure for selling and departing.

Considerations: While selling to a partner likely results in little disruption to the business, a near-immediate sale and exit, the likelihood of a cash payout and, if desired and negotiated, post-sale involvement as a board member or advisor, it seldom results in the highest possible selling price.

Option 2. Partially Selling to a Key Employee or New Co-owner or Partner

A partial sale of the business requires a detailed business valuation, determining what percentage of ownership to sell, drawing up legally binding partnership and buy-sell agreements, and becoming a co-owner or partner rather than the sole owner of the business.

Considerations: A partial sale allows owner flexibility in determining future business involvement and provides continuity for staff and clients. Especially if the partial sale is to a key employee, it rarely results in a top-dollar sale price and probably results in payments made over coming years.

Option 3. Selling to Another Business

Businesses or private equity groups acquire businesses, in full or in part, for strategic rather than purely financial reasons, most often to expand capabilities, market reach, competitiveness, and profitability. This is accomplished through integrating the offerings of the purchased business into those of the established business, which is usually larger and stronger than the business being purchased.

Considerations: A business-to-business sale allows for the possibility of a strong selling price and immediate payoff, though sale terms often require the seller's ongoing involvement in the business for a designated period of time.

Option 4. Partially Selling to Another Business

Selling a portion of your business to another business forms a strategic partnership with a business partner that can result in greater financial, operational, distribution, or marketing strength.

Considerations: A business partnership can be structured to include a succession plan that gradually sells the entirety of one business to the partner business. As in any partnership, this approach requires a detailed valuation and legally binding agreements that

2: Defining What You Want Out of Your Business Sale

specify terms and timelines.

Option 5. Transitioning to Next-Generation Family Members

This sale approach is the choice of as many as one in every three business owners. It rarely results in a top-dollar payoff, but, by passing ownership to an heir or heirs, the business stays in the family, the seller often has flexibility to determine post-transition involvement, and staff and clients usually experience the least disruption.

Considerations: This is an easy plan to consider and a complicated one to arrange. It requires consultation with attorneys and accountants to establish the valuation, create business transfer plans, and address tax- and estate-planning issues. If there is more than one able and interested heir, it also requires deciding which will assume business control and how others will be included in the transition plan – usually by transferring some of the business value and therefore a portion of the owner's wealth to the others, even if they don't attain business ownership.

Option 6. Selling to Employees

This approach involves a tax-qualified, defined employee benefit plan, called an employee stock ownership plan, or ESOP, through which employees buy or otherwise accumulate shares of the business quickly or over time, depending on how the plan is structured. It provides tax advantages, a phase-out of owner involvement, and continuity for staff and clients.

Considerations: An ESOP requires the involvement of an ESOP attorney. It also requires an employee or group of employees capable of taking over the business and ongoing involvement of the owner over the period, often years, between when the ESOP transfer begins and when the employee or employees assume full ownership.

Option 7. Selling to an Individual Buyer

This approach is the primary focus of the rest of this guide. It involves selling to someone who wants to buy rather than start a business, in part to avoid start-up risk and to benefit from established systems, products, staff, clientele, sales, and cash flow. Also, because many business sales involve seller financing — basically a seller-financed loan accompanied by an often-sizable down payment and a secured promissory note — those seeking a business for sale realize that it's often easier to finance a business purchase than to undertake a business start-up.

Considerations: Businesses with strong earnings and with sale terms that include seller financing are more likely to result in successful sales and higher prices. If your business is in strong condition and attractive to buyers, selling to an individual provides the greatest opportunity to achieve a timely sale at a good price and, possibly, post-sale involvement with the business — should that be of interest to you and the buyer.

Option 8. Liquidating

Liquidation is last on this list because it's often a last resort and always the lowest-value exit approach. It involves selling all tangible assets that can be converted to cash (including furnishings, fixtures, equipment, and inventory), collecting outstanding receivables, paying off debts, addressing contractual obligations, formally releasing employees, dealing with legal and financial obligations, and closing up shop.

Considerations: Liquidation results in no compensation for the goodwill or going concern value of a business. It becomes the exit option when the sale value of a business is the same or nearly the same as the sale value of its physical assets, or if the owner wants or needs an immediate exit from a low-value business and can't devote the time to plan and implement the value-enhancements outlined in Chapter 3.

2: Defining What You Want Out of Your Business Sale

> ### Step 3: Key Takeaways
> Depending on the circumstances, urgency, and financial expectations that motivate your exit, there are at least eight ways to sell your business:
> - Sell your part of the business to an existing partner
> - Sell a portion of the business to a key employee or new co-owner or partner
> - Sell to another business
> - Sell part of your business to another business
> - Transition ownership of your business to family members
> - Sell your business to your employees
> - Sell your business to an individual
> - Sell only tangible, physical assets and close the business

Step 4: Setting Your Top Exit Priority

After considering what is motivating you to exit from your business, and after resolving the potential conflicts among the objectives you hope to achieve, you need to weigh what, above all else, you most want out of your business exit.

By stating your highest priority, you aren't ruling out your other sale objectives. You're acknowledging that in order to achieve what you most want out of your exit, you may need to compromise on other aims.

It's time to check one box: Which one of the following objectives is your single highest exit priority?

- ❏ An immediate departure.
- ❏ The highest price possible.
- ❏ All-cash payoff at closing.
- ❏ Post-sale involvement with your business.
- ❏ Post-sale priorities such as little or no disruption to clients or staff.
- ❏ Pre-sale preparation followed by a future sale.

With your overarching goal in mind, you're in position to develop your exit plan and prepare your business for the sale in front of you,

BizBuySell Guide to SELLING YOUR BUSINESS

all covered in Chapter 3.

Key Terms

ESOP: Short for Employee Stock Ownership Plan, a tax-qualified defined employee benefit plan through which employees buy or otherwise accumulate shares of the business quickly or over time, depending on how the plan is structured, allowing tax advantages and a phase-out of owner involvement over time.

Seller Financing: An arrangement through which the buyer pays an often-sizable portion of the purchase price at closing and signs a promissory note to pay the seller the rest of the price, with interest, over a specified time period.

Valuable Online Resources

For additional resources on developing an exit strategy, go to bizbuysell.com and visit the BizBuySell Learning Center at https://www.bizbuysell.com/learning-center/.

Digital Toolkit Resources

Access the digital toolkit by visiting https://www.bizbuysell.com/seller/guide/selling-a-business/.

Motivations and Timing Worksheet
Prioritizing Sale Objectives Worksheet
Conflicting Objectives Worksheet

3

Planning Your Exit and Building Pre-Sale Business Value

Chapter 1 helped you arrive at a rough estimate of what your business is worth in its current condition.

Chapter 2 helped you define what is motivating your exit and what you want out of your business sale. It detailed the most common sale approaches and helped you consider each one against the sale terms and conditions you aim to achieve. Then it helped you consider your exit motivations, resolve conflicting objectives, and establish your primary exit goal.

This chapter helps you establish the exit strategy you will follow as you prepare to leave your business and capture its value through a sale. It guides you through the assessment of your business as a purchase prospect and helps you make decisions about the pre-sale condition of your business and the value enhancements necessary to achieve the sale you're aiming for.

Step by step and with worksheets in the Digital Toolkit, this chapter describes:

- How to set your exit plan.
- What buyers want, value, and seek in a business purchase.

- How to identify and plan value-enhancing business improvements.
- How pre-sale decisions can enhance sale value and minimize tax impact.

Step 1: Formulating Your Exit Strategy

The first step in exit planning is to establish the outcome you seek to achieve through the sale of your business.

Your Sale Goal

What is your desired sale outcome?

- To sell your business in part and remain involved with its operation.
- To sell your business in full and remain involved with its operation.
- To sell your business in full and end involvement with its operation, either immediately or after a transition period.

Your Timing Objective

For what exit timeframe are you aiming?

- Immediate (0-6 months).
- Within a year.
- Within 2-3 or more years.

Your Financial Objective

Most businesses sell at a multiple of what is called seller's discretionary earnings or owner's cash flow, which is another way of saying how much the business earns annually for its owner. The earnings multiple is based on the condition and attractiveness of the business. Businesses in weakest condition sell at a multiple of 1 or less, if at all, and businesses in strongest condition sell at a multiple of 5, or even higher.

Based on the condition of your business and the urgency of your timing, what is your financial expectation?

- My business is in strong condition and likely to command a high earnings multiple.
- I am prepared to accept a lower price due to my timing urgency and the current condition of my business.
- I am willing to commit time and effort to strengthen my business condition and therefore improve its likely attractiveness and earnings multiple.

Your Pay-Out Objective

Will you require all-cash at closing or are you willing to offer a seller-financed loan, realizing that all-cash closings most often result in lower sale prices and, because a third-party loan is likely necessary, a slower sale closing.

- I am willing to provide a seller-financed loan for a portion of the sale price.
- I will require an all-cash payoff at closing.

Your Sale-Marketing Objective

Have you defined your preferred buyer, or are you interested in selling to any qualified buyer, whether a business or an individual?

- I prefer or am obligated to sell to a partner, key employee, employee group, or family member. (If so, you will not need to list or market your business for sale. Instead, you will work with legal and financial advisors as you pursue next steps.)
- I intend to pursue a sale to a targeted business such as a supplier, competitor, or strategic business buyer. (If so, you will not need to list your business for sale. Instead, you will work with legal and financial advisors as you strategically market your business to select targets.)
- I seek to sell to any buyer who has the necessary financial, expertise, and management capability to buy my business. (If so, proceed with the following parts of this guide as you prepare to list, market, and sell your business.)

Your Personal Post-Sale Objective

- I want to stay involved with my business after its sale, in a managerial capacity or as a consultant or board member.
- I am willing to remain involved over a post-sale transition period of 1-3 months or longer.
- I prefer to end my relationship with the business upon completion of the sale.

Your Post-Sale Objective for Your Business

- I prefer to sell to a buyer who plans to retain employees and to cause little disruption to staff, clients, or customers of the business.
- I am willing to sell to a buyer who plans to merge, move, or significantly alter the business.

Put your objectives in writing. You may decide to make adjustments to your desired outcomes after completing the Step 2 assessment of the condition of your business and after determining the extent of pre-sale improvements you want to make, but the objectives you set at the outset will provide the starting point you will plan from.

> ### Step 1: Key Takeaways
>
> Your exit strategy is guided by your sale objectives:
>
> - The extent of pre-sale improvements required to enhance business attractiveness and value may guide your decision to reassess either your timing objective or your financial expectations.
> - The condition of your business as an attractive sale prospect, your desired exit timing, your sale pay-out objective, and your after-sale requirements may affect your financial expectations.
> - The extent of pre-sale improvements required to achieve your desired price, unless you reduce your price expectations, may affect your timing expectations.
> - Preference for a certain kind of buyer will affect how you market your business for sale, which will begin with a sale listing only if you have no buyer preferences beyond a buyer who has the financial and managerial capacity to buy the business.

3: Planning Your Exit and Building Pre-Sale Business Value

Step 2: Understanding What Business Buyers Want

After getting a sense of what your business is currently worth, covered in Chapter 1, if you are like most owners your next question has to do with whether your business can actually be sold.

While each buyer seeks a specific type of business, perhaps based on location, business sector, or even business size, all buyers seek businesses with strength in the conditions listed in this section. Businesses that gain the highest ratings in all areas sell for the highest prices, while those with good-to-medium conditions sell at lower prices, and those with poor conditions likely are not considered as purchase prospects without significant pre-sale improvements, which are covered in Step 3.

- **Strong revenues and profits:** When buyers evaluate businesses, money talks first and loudest. They are looking for increasing sales, increasing profits, and, especially, strong owner earnings. Owner earnings become the basis of the business valuation, with higher earnings leading to higher business prices. They are also important because most buyers want to know that any business they consider can provide strong annual earnings for its owner.

- **Strong financial condition:** Buyers want to review financial statements that go back at least three years to verify the following conditions:
  - Positive cash flow, resulting from more money flowing into the business than transferring out of the business.
  - Working capital, which is the positive difference between the current assets of the business and its current liabilities.
  - All taxes paid to date.
  - Either no debt or current debt payments.
  - Current accounts receivable.
  - Assets that exceed liabilities.

- **Clear legal condition:** Buyers avoid businesses with legal issues, or signals that legal issues lie ahead in the form of lawsuits, contract disputes, or pending legal actions, whether from product warranties, employee lawsuits, regulation or zoning issues, or any other unaddressed legal issues.

- **Distinct and competitive products and services:** Buyers are attracted to businesses with products and services that are in strong demand and that generate steadily increasing revenues and profits. They value products that are produced using proprietary or difficult-to-replicate processes that serve as a barrier to competition but are well documented for easy adoption by a new owner.

- **Location:** Buyers seek businesses that are well positioned geographically and within industries or business sectors that are strong and growing.

  They value an attractive geographic location for livability, for accessibility, and, if your business serves a local clientele or relies on a local workforce, for access to a growing population of residents who match the customer profile and employee descriptions of your business. They also seek businesses with attractive physical facilities located in areas with no threat of zoning, redevelopment, or other changes that could threaten business viability.

- **Facilities and Equipment:** Buyers value modern facilities and equipment that is either owned outright by the business or on long-term, transferable leases. They also expect equipment to be in sound condition, and backed by transferable service contracts.

- **Capabilities and Processes:** Buyers seek businesses with systems in place to achieve financial goals and keep the business running smoothly. These include well-structured and cost-efficient operations that are well documented and implemented, strong marketing, customer service that draws good reviews and word-of-mouth, and, depending on the nature of the business, other capabilities such as distribution

3: Planning Your Exit and Building Pre-Sale Business Value

and delivery and research and development.
- **Staffing:** Buyers want assurance that the business success does not rely solely on the current owner's management, skills, and knowledge. They prefer businesses with an organizational structure that supports business success even in the owner's absence, with key managers who can provide continuity after the sale.

  They want to know that key managers have signed employee contracts and enjoy benefits that heighten the likelihood they will remain with the business after the sale to ease a smooth transition to a new owner. And they want assurance that staff is well trained, with employment policies outlined in an employee manual or handbook.

- **Clientele:** Buyers want assurance that the clients or customers of the business rely on and value the offerings of the business and the expertise of its managers and staff as much or even more than they rely on the owner's personal expertise and interaction. Put differently, they want to know business success does not hinge on the current owner's presence and abilities.

  They want to see that the business has a loyal clientele (unless its success relies on transactional rather than long-term or repeat customers), a broad client roster rather than reliance on a few customers, signed long-term contracts with major clients, and a well-maintained client database.

- **Brand and Reputation:** Almost any buyer with interest in a business quickly conducts an online search. Buyers want verification that the business they are considering is well regarded, well known, respected in its market area and business sector, and backed by positive customer relations, strong marketing, and a positive online presence.

  They want assurance that the business has a strong and respected brand and, as the owner of the business, you want the same thing, because a strong brand and positive reputation contribute heavily to the intangible value of your business – to its goodwill – which is a strong contributor to the value of the business and the price a buyer will pay.

- **Transferability:** Buyers seek assurance that the business can transfer with no obstacles, including:
  - Transferability of clients: Buyers need to know that customers, especially major customers, are committed to and served by the business and not just its owner, and that contracts and a well-maintained client database will transfer with the business purchase.
  - Transferability of business capabilities and processes: Buyers value processes and systems that are well defined, well documented, and easy to adopt.
  - Transferability of business contracts: Buyers expect well documented and transferable relationships with customers, suppliers, distributors and other key associates, and transferable long-term leases on facilities and equipment.
  - Transferability of workforce: Buyers want to see that key employees have contracts, employee benefit plans, and other incentives that keep them loyal to the business.

Step 2: Key Takeaways

Buyers seek businesses with strength in the following areas:

- Revenue and profits
- Financial condition
- Legal condition
- Location
- Facilities and equipment
- Capabilities and processes
- Staffing
- Clientele
- Brand and reputation
- Ease of transferability to a new owner

3: Planning Your Exit and Building Pre-Sale Business Value

Step 3: Assessing Your Business as a Purchase Prospect

Use the **Business Condition Assessment Worksheet in the Digital Toolkit** as you assess the current condition of your business against the strengths that buyers seek when considering a business purchase.

Your answers to the worksheet's Yes/No questions will help you assess the sale-readiness of your business in each of the 10 areas buyers examine. It will also help you prioritize improvement needs and estimate the timeframe required to make improvements.

If you answer Yes to all questions on the worksheet, your business is in sale-ready condition. If not – if you are like most owners and answer No to some or many questions – you have three exit options:

- Make the decision to liquidate assets and close rather than attempt to sell the business – the decision of owners with urgent need for an immediate exit and business conditions in high need of pre-sale improvement.
- Make business and value enhancements before offering your business at the price you aim to achieve.
- Reduce your price expectations and offer the business in as-is or slightly improved condition.
- Before a sale offering, assess the condition of your business against the strengths that buyers seek, then prioritize and estimate the time required for improvement needs.

> **Step 3: Key Takeaways**
>
> Business condition affects pricing and exit-timing expectations:
>
> - To achieve your target price, you may need to extend your exit timing objective to allow for condition and value enhancements before offering your business for sale.
> - To offer your business as-is or only slightly enhanced condition, you may need to reduce your price expectations before offering it for sale.
> - As a last resort, a business in high need of improvement and an owner with an urgent exit-timing objective may decide to liquidate assets and close rather than attempt to sell the business.

Step 4: Identifying Pre-Sale Improvements to Attract Buyers and Build Value

Pre-Sale Improvement Objectives

Two objectives guide pre-sale improvement plans:

- **Enhance strengths** that most contribute to the attractiveness and value of your business. For example, financial condition is a strength every buyer seeks. If the cash flow of your business is weak, or even if it is in good but not great condition, aim to make it a high target for pre-sale improvement.
- **Overcome weaknesses** that most detract from the attractiveness and value of your business. For example, reliance on only a few clients, or lack of key staff who will continue after the sale, are viewed by buyers as purchase deterrents and therefore weaknesses. These should be high targets to address during for pre-sale planning.

If your exit timeframe allows, plan to address every condition that you ranked as being in high need of improvement when you completed the Business Condition Assessment Worksheet in Step 3.

Two objectives guide pre-sale improvement plans: Enhance strengths that most contribute to the attractiveness and value of your business, and overcome weaknesses that most detract from the attractiveness and value of your business.

If your exit timeframe is short, plan at least to address every condition that you believe a buyer will view as a major strength or a major weakness. The upcoming sections detail improvements to consider.

Pre-Sale Improvement Actions

Following your pre-sale assessment of the condition of your business, consider the recommended actions in this section as you plan to address any improvement needs.

To develop sales and profits, work with your management team or a consultant as you consider the following actions:

- Assess how the sales and profits of your business have trended over the past three years, using the **Sales and Profit Growth Chart in the Digital Toolkit.**
- Review your business model, which is a description of how your business makes money. Analyze whether there are revenue sources that could be developed, for example online sales, sales of accessory items, or service agreements, and, if so, consider a reallocation of business resources to those areas.
- Identify purchase patterns or successful marketing campaigns you may be able to build upon or replicate. Also, identify seasonality patterns that provide opportunity to increase production, pricing, and sales.
- Determine if you can reduce cost of sales, and therefore increase profit margins, perhaps through bulk purchases, diversifying suppliers, and reworking or diversifying supplier contracts, which may also lower supply-chain risks.
- Reassess pricing, increasing margins or rates on your high-demand unique offerings and adjusting prices, based on competitive research, to win either more sales or greater margin on widely available offerings.
- Look for areas in your business where you have capacity to grow.
- Identify which products or services deliver the lowest- and highest-profit margins and decide whether you can shift sales emphasis from one to the other.
- Develop streams of recurring revenue, automatically repeating sales or, for service businesses, service contracts. These provide revenue predictability, lower marketing costs, and high

attractiveness to buyers.

In addition to strengthening revenues and profits prior to your sale offering, be aware that buyers want to see key areas of growth potential, and therefore revenue potential. Be ready to highlight areas where your business is not currently at full capacity, and therefore areas that present opportunity for the new owner to experience business growth.

To strengthen the financial condition of your business, work with your management team and accountant to consider the following actions:

- Optimize accounts receivable by promptly following up with past-due invoices, creating payment plans for late-paying customers, and introducing incentives for early payments and penalties for late payments.
- Negotiate terms for accounts payable, including early payment discounts and/or longer payment cycles.
- Reduce expenses by eliminating unnecessary purchases, renegotiating vendor pricing where possible, or shopping for less-expensive alternatives.
- Reassess inventory needs, buying less if stocks are sufficient and renegotiating or shopping for better or bulk pricing for future purchases.
- Consider seeking a small business line of credit to preserve cash flow.

To present necessary financial statements for the past three years, work with your CPA to prepare the following:

- An income statement, also called a profit and loss statement.
- A balance sheet, which presents the financial condition of the business.
- A seller's discretionary earnings (SDE) statement, which recasts the income statement into a pro forma estimate of how much money the business generates annually for the benefit of its owner. This is also called an adjusted cash flow statement or a

3: Planning Your Exit and Building Pre-Sale Business Value

statement of recast earnings. It is of primary interest to a buyer.

While the income statement reflects deductions for every allowable business expense and legitimately minimizes profits and taxes, the SDE statement is a recast or "normalized" income statement that adds back deductions for interest, depreciation, taxes and amortization, one-time expenses, expenses (including salary) that benefit the owner directly, and discretionary expenses another owner might not choose to incur. The result is a bottom line that reflects how much the owner earns or benefits annually from the business.

To address unresolved issues that affect the legal condition of your business, seek legal advice as you examine and plan to address the following issues:

- Patents that will be part of the business sale must be current, not nearing expiration dates, and owned by the business and not by the owner personally.
- The lease for the business location must be current, assignable, and transferable. If the location is essential to the ongoing success of the business, it should extend at least five years into the future, ideally with lease increases protected by rate-escalation clauses.
- The business must be clear of any zoning-regulation violations. If there are pending regulations or grandfathered variances that a sale may void, be prepared to disclose these facts rather than have them discovered during due diligence.
- Any legal claims, encumbrances, or liens against the business should be cleared prior to the sale offering.
- Pending or unresolved lawsuits must be concluded before the sale or disclosed early in the selling process, long before due diligence discovery.
- If your business has faced or faces employee-related issues, be prepared to disclose the problems and outline the steps taken to preclude similar issues in the future.
- If your business has had regulation or law violations, or

environmental or safety compliance issues, the expenses will be yours to address. Additionally, the risk must be overcome, or you should be prepared to assure the buyer of controls that will avoid recurrence of the violations.
- Be sure all licenses are up to date.
- Be sure any necessary third-party consents to your sale will be easily obtained.

As a key step in preparing for legal due diligence, you will also need to assemble all the documentation the buyer and buyer's advisors will require. Use the **Business Sale Documentation Checklist in the Digital Toolkit,** along with advice from your attorney and broker, if you are using one, as you compile the necessary information.

To strengthen the marketing of the products and services of your business, consider the following actions:

- Be prepared to present how your products and services are decidedly better and preferred when compared to competing options.
- Be prepared to present how your products and services are produced using a process that is difficult to copy but easy to adopt and follow.
- Review and improve product presentation and packaging to enhance visual appeal and to reduce cost, waste and environmental impact.
- Improve and document proprietary production processes.
- Consider creation of automatic purchase programs, complementary products that provide new streams of revenue, and bulk or repeat purchase incentives.
- Study online reviews for your business and products. Especially if existing reviews are dated or less-than sterling, cultivate new reviews by personally inviting your best customers to share their opinions. Provide the URLs of sites prospective buyers will likely check, taking care not to violate review site rules by offering payment for good reviews, inspiring negative reviews

3: Planning Your Exit and Building Pre-Sale Business Value

of competitors, or posting reviews misrepresenting yourself.

To strengthen or overcome conditions that weaken your business location, consider the following actions:

- If your business relies on its local market for customers, and if those customers are showing declining interest in the products or services of your business, consider product revisions to increase appeal. Also consider product and marketing adjustments that attract new customers from the local market, from nearby markets, and from markets that might be served remotely.
- If your business relies on the local market for staffing and finds employee recruitment increasingly difficult, review the competitiveness of the salaries, benefits, and conditions your business offers, while also considering how a remote work force could compensate for the availability of local market employees.
- If your business sector or industry faces regulatory, legal, or growth challenges, consider how you can shift the emphasis of your business and its offerings away from high-risk aspects and toward undamaged niches of the industry.
- If your business has not adapted to recent industry changes, plan to make necessary adjustments to bring it into alignment with industry standards prior to a sale offering.
- If your business location attracts foot traffic, review and update business signage, point of entry, and interior, ensuring that it is clean and in condition to make a strong first impression.

Local business groups and industry associations are resources to tap as you make pre-sale adjustments. Showing membership in such groups enhances business attractiveness, both by demonstrating market and industry involvement and by creating positive connections with those a buyer may contact while forming impressions about your business as a purchase prospect.

To make improvements to the facilities and equipment of your business, consider the following actions:

- See that all equipment is in good order and ready for presentation, not only through a facility tour but also in the form of an asset list that itemizes furnishings and equipment either by type — such as office furniture, computers, production equipment, and so forth — or by the way they are used in your business. Use the **Asset Valuation Worksheet in the Digital Toolkit** as you create your list.
- If equipment is owned rather than leased, confirm that it is owned by the business and not the owner, and that titles are free of liens or encumbrances.
- If equipment is leased, review the stipulations, length, and transferability of contracts.
- See that all manuals, leases, service contracts and other supporting documents are ready for presentation.

To strengthen the capabilities and processes of your business, consider the following actions:

- Define the capabilities that most contribute to the success of your business, for example product production, sales, customer service, and the processes involved with each.
- See that business processes are detailed in process manuals.
- Write or update your business plan and create a short-form version that presents an overview of the business, its mission statement, key products or services, its business model, and business goals and objectives.
- Write or update your marketing plan and create a short-form version that describes your market situation, market position, brand statement, and strategies for products, distribution, pricing, and advertising and promotions.

To strengthen the management and staffing of your business, consider the following actions:

- Create and train a management team that is committed to the business, backed by solid training and transferable employment

3: Planning Your Exit and Building Pre-Sale Business Value

contracts. This increases the likelihood that management team members will stay with the business after the sale and contribute to a successful ownership transition.
- Create employment policies that are outlined in an employee manual or handbook that brings together employment and job-related information and clarifies policies.
- Create an organization chart or a description of your business organization and structure that will reinforce your plan for an easy ownership transition.
- Document your personal role and responsibilities in the business and, if necessary, create a plan to shift responsibilities to key managers or staff who are likely to remain with the business after the sale.

To strengthen the clientele, client relations, and client databases of your business, consider the following actions:
- Review the condition of your customer database, or create one if necessary, and update entries so they are current at the time of business transition.
- With your attorney, review current client contracts for accuracy and transferability.
- If necessary, reduce reliance on one or a few clients by developing a broader customer base.
- If necessary, reduce the reliance of key customers on your personal presence and interaction by developing their relationships with and confidence in key managers or staff members.

To strengthen the brand and reputation of your business, consider the following actions:
- See that your website is well designed, well optimized for search, quick to load, and owned not by you, personally, or by its designer, but by the business and therefore transferable as part of the sale.

- If you have not done so already, secure your business name with your state's business filing agency, and also secure it online as a domain name and across social media channels.
- Unify your business identity across all signage, displays, advertising and sales materials.
- Review search results and create a plan for generating positive reviews and publicity, if needed.

> **Step 4: Key Takeaways**
>
> Pre-sale business improvements accomplish two objectives:
> - Enhance the most valuable business strengths to achieve greatest business attractiveness and value.
> - Overcome or minimize the greatest weaknesses that most detract from business strength and attractiveness.
>
> Pre-sale business improvements require commitment and confidentiality:
> - Commit the necessary resources and assign tasks, deadlines, and responsibilities.
> - Share sale intentions only as necessary and with a strong request for confidentiality to avoid devaluing your business by creating unnecessary staff or customer uncertainty.

Step 5: Making Pre-Sale Decisions That Impact Sale Value and Taxes

Before listing your business for sale, work with your accountant or financial advisor to weigh the impact of how the sale you are planning will be structured and financed.

Sale Structure

Business sales are structured as asset sales or as entity sales. All sales of sole proprietorships must be structured as asset sales, but businesses that are incorporated or formed as LLCs can also be structured as entity sales.

3: Planning Your Exit and Building Pre-Sale Business Value

- **An entity sale** transfers the entire business including all its assets and all its liabilities except those specifically listed as exclusions.
- **An asset sale** transfers only the tangible and intangible assets, except those listed as exclusions, into a new business formed by the buyer.

Most buyers prefer deals structured as asset sales to avoid the transfer of liabilities. Most sellers prefer entity sales for these reasons:

- **Entity sale proceeds are taxed at the capital gains rate**, which is currently considerably lower than proceeds taxed as ordinary income.
- **In an entity sale, liabilities transfer to the buyer** unless they are specifically excluded. This eliminates the seller's risk of future responsibility for liabilities which, in an asset sale, would remain with the seller.

Sale structure becomes an issue for buyer-seller negotiation and is covered fully in Chapter 7. During exit planning, however, it is useful to have an early understanding of the topic as you establish sale objectives.

Seller Financing

All sources concur that business sale listings that offer seller financing – requiring a good portion of the purchase price at closing and receiving the balance, plus interest, over a specified period of time – achieve higher asking-to-closing prices. As you consider a sale, discuss with your financial advisors the upsides, downsides, and tax advantages of offering seller financing.

Upsides of Seller Financing

- Buyers prefer seller financing
  - It eases their concern about your confidence in the future success of your business.
  - It reduces their need to seek third-party loans.
  - It provides more flexible payment terms than those offered

through most bank loans.
- It involves no loan origination or other fees.
- It allows the buyer to pay for the purchase in part at closing and the remainder over coming years.
- Sellers benefit from seller financing:
  - It attracts more buyer interest and higher purchase offers.
  - It spreads sale income and therefore the tax impact from the sale over a number of years.
  - It involves a seller-to-buyer loan that provides interest income in addition to sale income.

Downsides of Seller Financing

- The buyer can default on payment obligations—a not uncommon outcome. Especially if the buyer has weak business experience and poor financial expertise, the condition of the business can falter during the post-sale period, with loan payments being one of the first casualties. For that reason, it is essential to secure the loan with protections described in Chapter 7.
- Foreclosure clauses do not protect against business devaluation, which occurs if the buyer depletes inventory and devalues assets by the time the business lands back in the seller's hands, underscoring the need for conducting due diligence and obtaining strong personal guarantees and loan security prior to seller-financing agreements.

Financial and Tax Implications

- A request for an all-cash payoff at closing often results in fewer offers and lower sale prices, and it also results in the receipt of all sale income in a single year, likely pushing the seller into a higher tax bracket and reducing net proceeds from the sale.

3: Planning Your Exit and Building Pre-Sale Business Value

> **Step 5: Key Takeaways**
>
> **Pre-sale considerations have tax and value impact:** Seller-financing and the structure of a business sale can result in sale implications worthy of early advice from an accounting or financial advisor.
> - Whether a sale is structured as an asset sale (the only structure available in the sale of a sole proprietorship) or as an entity sale becomes a point of negotiation because one structure is more appealing to buyers and the other is more appealing and offers tax advantages to sellers.
> - Whether the seller requires an all-cash payoff at closing or offers seller financing impacts the attractiveness of the offer, the selling price, and when proceeds are taxed.

Key Terms

Asset Sale: A sale in which the seller keeps the actual, legal business structure, called the business entity, and sells only tangible and intangible business assets, which the buyer moves to a newly formed business entity. An asset sale is the only approach available to sole proprietors, who have no stock to sell. It is the preferred sale structure of buyers, who avoid risk by buying the assets of the business and assuming only select and specified liabilities.

Entity Sale: Also called a stock sale. A sale in which the owner of a corporation sells its stock, or the owner of an LLC sells its membership shares, to a new owner. With the sale of stock or membership shares, the seller transfers and the buyer assumes all business assets and liabilities that are not specifically excluded from the transaction.

Sale Structure: The legal manner in which a business is sold, either through an entity sale, which is also called a stock sale, or through an asset sale. Each sale approach has tax and liability implications that merit early counsel from your attorney and accountant.

BizBuySell Guide to SELLING YOUR BUSINESS

Digital Toolkit Resources

Access the digital toolkit by visiting https://www.bizbuysell.com/seller/guide/selling-a-business/.

Business Condition Assessment Worksheet
Sales and Profit Growth Chart
Business Sale Documentation Checklist
Asset Valuation Worksheet

Part II
Attracting Buyers and Selling Your Business

4

Launching the Sale of Your Business

You have arrived at a good estimate of what your business is worth (Chapter 1). You have examined your motivations, objectives and preferred outcomes (Chapter 2). You have assessed the current condition of your business as a sale prospect, set your exit strategy, and enhanced the value of your business to make it more attractive to buyers (Chapter 3).

You are ready to exit your business. It is time to launch the sale process.

This chapter guides you through the sale-planning steps in front of you:

- Assembling your business sale team.
- Compiling financial records and necessary documents.
- Finalizing your sale asking price.
- Preparing your business story – in summary form and in a selling memorandum.
- Creating your business-for-sale listing.
- Marketing your business to potential buyers.

Step 1: Assembling Your Business Sale Team

Every step in this chapter is essential to business sale success, and perhaps none is more important than your selection of professionals who will guide and assist you through the selling process. Nearly all sale teams include an accountant and an attorney and many also rely on the expertise of a business broker — an experienced professional with the skills and resources to maintain confidentiality while guiding you through the process from sale pricing to marketing to negotiation to closing the sale and transferring the business.

It is impossible to overstate the value of experienced advisors in a business sale. No owner, no matter how small the business or how seemingly uncomplicated the sale deal, should sell without, at the very least, first seeking financial and tax advice.

In addition to the necessary expertise of an accountant and an attorney, many owners also rely on a business broker, and, depending on unique circumstances, others also seek input from appraisers, valuation experts, and business consultants.

Deciding Which Advisors to Include on Your Business Sale Team

While you alone make the decision to sell your business, every step after that decision benefits from professional advice.

Which advisors you select for your team depends on the nature of your business, your personal marketing and negotiating capabilities, and the time you can devote to the selling effort. Business sale-team advisors include:

- **CPAs or accountants**, especially ones who have experience with sales of businesses of your size and type, deliver essential advice throughout the sale process. They provide valuable assistance formulating preliminary valuations of the assets and goodwill of your business, setting the sale price, preparing financial statements, reviewing business tax filings, estimating and mitigating tax liabilities, structuring the deal, assisting during the buyer's due diligence, and also conducting due diligence, on the buyer's financial condition and ability to complete the purchase. They also provide essential expertise when assessing and weighing the tax impact of buyer price negotiations and throughout the closing process.

- **An attorney** provides essential advice during sale preparation, due diligence, buyer-seller negotiations, and sale closing. Even the smallest and least-complicated business sale should involve the advice of an attorney experienced in selling businesses. Long before the necessary task of drafting or reviewing the purchase and sale agreement and other paperwork, your attorney will assist in reviewing the condition of contracts, leases, loans, and other legal obligations of your business, reviewing and negotiating the buyer's purchase offer, and providing advice regarding legal ramifications from issues that arise during sale negotiations.
- **A broker** provides valuable advice and assistance while helping to maintain necessary confidentiality through every step of the sale process — preparation, pricing, marketing, due diligence, negotiation and closing. The broker's role is especially important for business owners who have limited experience in selling, whose buyer pool is broad and difficult to reach, and who lack time to both run the business and sell the business without endangering the strength of the business.
- **Consultants** can assist in overcoming business challenges by providing insight and experience to improve business strategy, marketing, finances, operations, management, technology, or other aspects of the business. They are especially valuable when the business selling price could be significantly higher with major business improvements beyond the expertise of the

business owner and management team, and when the owner has a generous pre-sale preparation timeframe for improving processes, organization, marketing, sales, and use of business resources.
- **An appraiser or valuation expert** is necessary for a business with difficult-to-assess intellectual property, proprietary processes, a valuable brand, other high-value intangible assets, or real property. (Some brokers provide appraisal assistance, but be aware that many buyers, when considering businesses with high-value intangible assets, consider only valuations by credentialed appraisers. See the upcoming section titled "Selecting an Appraiser.")

Determining Whether and How to Hire a Business Broker

Businesses marketed by their owners rather than by brokers are called "for sale by owner" or FSBO (pronounced "fizbo"), exactly as you see in the housing real estate market.

Typically, business owners go the FSBO route if:

- They cannot find a broker interested in representing the business for sale.
- They don't want to pay the broker's commission, also called a success fee, which is normally a percentage of the final purchase price and may vary depending on brokerage, deal size, and structure.
- They want to maintain complete control and feel they can handle the process themselves.

Even if you can go it alone, before opting for that route, consider the role brokers play:

- They serve as advisors with in-depth insights on valuation, marketing, prospecting, negotiations, and other fundamental sale elements.
- They can ensure confidentially while marketing your business to qualified buyer prospects.
- Most have extensive prior business experience and understanding

of the financial, operational, and legal issues of selling and transitioning businesses.
- They facilitate and streamline the selling process, allowing the owner to focus on operating the business.

Selecting Your Business Broker

Although there is some crossover, and some brokers serve businesses of all sizes, most brokers fit into two categories:

- Businesses worth more than $2 million dollars are usually sold by mergers and acquisitions (M&A) specialists.
- Smaller businesses typically work with main street business brokers.

When seeking a qualified broker to help sell your business, search the BizBuySell Broker Directory at https://www.bizbuysell.com/business-brokers/, which includes thousands of qualified professionals.

When interviewing brokers, base comparisons on the following factors:

- **Credentials & Training:**
  - Is the broker a certified business intermediary (CBI) and member of the International Business Brokers Association (IBBA), a member of M&A Source, or a member of a state or regional broker association?
  - Is the broker licensed to sell businesses in your state? Many states require a real estate license.
  - Does the broker have other credentials or training, for example CPA, MBA, or other professional certifications?

- **Experience:**
  - How long has the broker been in business?
  - Does the broker work full time or part time?
  - Does the broker work independently or as part of a broker group?
  - Does the broker have experience with businesses similar to yours?

- **Performance Record:**
  - How many listings does the broker have annually?

- How many annual sales?
- What is the average sale price compared to average asking price of the broker's recent annual sales?
- **Marketing Strength:**
  - How professional is the broker's site and is it well-optimized for search engines?
  - How many prospective buyers are in the broker's database?
- **Marketing Approach:**
  - How would the broker price your business?
  - How would your listing be marketed?
  - How does the broker use online business-for-sale listing sites, and which ones?
- **Contractual Arrangements:**
  - What is the broker's fee? (Broker fees are typically a percentage of the purchase price or a pre-set fee; whichever is greater.)
  - What is the length or term of the listing agreement? For example, 6 months, 12 months, 18 months.
  - Does the broker charge a cancellation fee if you withdraw the listing?
  - Does the broker charge a trailing fee if, after the listing agreement expires, you sell the business to a buyer who was referred by the broker?
- **References:**
  - Will the broker provide names and contact information so you can interview recent clients?

As you interview brokers, use the form titled **Broker Interview Notes in the Digital Toolkit**. It lists the questions to ask and provides space to record broker responses. Complete one form for each broker interview to make later comparisons easier. Access the digital toolkit by visiting https://www.bizbuysell.com/seller/guide/selling-a-business/.

Determining the Need for an Appraiser

If the price of your business will include the value of difficult-to-assess assets, plan to obtain a formal business appraisal that will hold up under the buyer's review during due diligence:

- **If your business owns valuable intangible assets**, including such assets as trademarks, patents, copyrights, trade secrets, proprietary processes, or a valuable brand, obtain valuation advice from a business appraiser and preferably one with a professional designation from a recognized trade association.

  Although your accountant or broker may be able to provide such an appraisal, especially if the assets have high value, to avoid buyer challenges or objections during due diligence, seek an appraiser with one of the following credentials:

  CBA - Certified Business Appraiser | ASA - Accredited Senior Appraiser | CPA/ABV - Certified Public Accountant Accredited in Business Valuations | CVA - Certified Valuation Analyst | CBV - Chartered Business Valuator.

- **If your business owns valuable real property**, seek assessment advice from a real estate appraiser.

Maintaining Confidentiality

Customers, competitors, suppliers, employees, and creditors will all react, and often against your interests, if they learn that your business is for sale. Even buyer prospects often have negative reactions if they learn a business opportunity hasn't been kept confidential.

Chapter 5 details how to protect confidentiality when dealing with prospects. However, even before listing your business and attracting buyer interest, work with your legal advisor to create confidentiality agreements for use when dealing with sale advisers and other confidants. Otherwise, you risk disturbing the confidence of your staff, suppliers, or customers, which is the last thing you want when you're working to keep your business value at its highest.

The **Mutual Confidentiality Agreement Sample Template in the Digital Toolkit** presents the conditions covered in most agreements.

> ### Step 1: Key Takeaways
>
> Business sale-team advisors include:
>
> - An accountant: Essential to provide financial and tax advice during sale preparation, pricing, due diligence, negotiations, and closing.
> - An attorney: Essential to provide legal counsel during sale preparation, due diligence, sale negotiations, and closure.
> - A broker: Important throughout the sale process, especially for owners who have limited sales experience, whose buyer pool is broad and difficult to reach, and who lack time to both run the business and sell the business without endangering business strength.
> - Consultants: Valuable when the business selling price could be significantly higher and when sellers have an exit time frame that allows for significant business improvements.
> - An appraiser: Important when business pricing includes intellectual property, proprietary processes, a valuable brand, other intangible assets, or real property. Brokers and accountants can often provide appraisal assistance but a credentialed appraiser with a professional designation from a recognized trade association is often required to reduce buyer challenges.
> - Confidentiality is essential throughout the sale process. Be prepared to obtain confidentiality agreements from sale advisers and other confidants.

Step 2: Compiling Financial Records and Necessary Documents

During the sale process your prospective buyer – and the buyer's accountant, attorney and legal counsel – will not only want but will require you to share facts about your business along with documents supporting your claims about the strength and health of your business. You need to be ready with:

- Professionally produced financial statements, records, and contracts.
- Facts and records that verify the condition of your business.

4: Launching the Sale of Your Business

- Confidentiality agreements to present for signature before divulging facts about your business.
- Business sale agreements and contracts.

CAUTION: Be sure financial statements are produced in accordance with generally accepted accounting principles (GAAP) and that all documents accurately represent the conditions of your business. Work with your financial and legal advisors in advance to make necessary pre-sale adjustments to avoid discrepancies that could be discovered during sale negotiations or due diligence, when they are most apt to upset the deal and most likely to cause price renegotiations and cost you more in legal and accounting fees.

Financial Condition Documentation

A buyer will require a full set of professionally produced financial documents that present the financial condition and financial trends of your business for the current and past several years, along with backup records that support your financial statements. Work with your accountant as you prepare to present the following:

- **Financial statements** for the year to date and the past two to three years, including income statements, balance sheets and cash flow statements. If your business owns assets that you want to exclude from the sale, for instance your automobile, seek advice from your accountant regarding the possible need to restate your balance sheet prior to the sale, at which time you will probably also remove any cash or investment accounts from the balance sheet, as those won't be part of the sale.
- **Seller's discretionary earnings (SDE) statements** for the past two to three years. Also called an adjusted cash flow statement, the SDE statement recasts the income statement to provide a pro forma estimate of how much the business generates annually for the benefit of its owner. Use the **SDE Calculation Worksheet in the Digital Toolkit** and work with your accountant as you prepare to present this information.
- **Three-year financial trends**, which can be presented in an at-a-glance chart using the **Sales and Profit Growth Chart in the**

65

Digital Toolkit.

- **Financial documentation** including accounts payable and accounts receivable aging reports, and the current ratio, also called the liquidity ratio, of your business. Depending on the nature of your business, you may also need to present your inventory turnover rate, which is an indicator of efficiency in manufacturing, distribution, and retail businesses.
- **Back-up records** that support the accuracy of your financial records, including bank statements and Corporate or Schedule C tax returns.

Business Condition Documentation

You'll need to assemble the preceding list of financial condition documentation before even listing your business, so that you'll be ready to meet with prospective buyers.

Later, as your sale proceeds to the due diligence and closing phases, you'll also need the following documentation. Although you can gather it later, be aware of what's required and begin to assemble the information early-on, so it's ready when you'll need it.

- Business formation documents, licenses, registrations, and certifications.
- Partnership or investor agreements, if any.
- Business licenses, certifications, and registrations.
- Professional certifications.
- Intellectual property ownership and valuation documents.
- Inventory list with value details.
- Listings of tangible assets, valuations, and depreciation schedules.
- Building and equipment leases and maintenance agreements.
- Contracts for major clients and for suppliers and distributors.
- Insurance policies.
- Information on outstanding loans and liens.
- Information on business operations including client lists, staffing lists, product and services lists with pricing, organization chart, employment policy manual, business plan, marketing plan, and procedures manual.

Legal Documents Required During the Sale Process

Be prepared with the legal documents you will need during the sale process, including the following:

- A non-disclosure confidentiality agreement (NDA), which sale confidants and prospective buyers will be required to sign before you divulge information about your business and its sale.
- A note for seller financing, which will be required if you plan to accept a portion of the business sale price over time and with interest, a condition that enhances most sale offerings and leads to higher asking-to-closing prices.
- A blank personal financial statement, which the buyer will be required to complete to allow verification of financial capability to make the business purchase.
- An offer-to-purchase agreement, which itemizes the price, assets, terms, and conditions involved in the upcoming sale and clarifies the rights, obligations and responsibilities of the buyer and the seller. Detailed in Chapter 7, in all but the simplest sales this agreement will be developed with advice from your broker or written by your attorney or the buyer's attorney.

CAUTION: Take this document-compilation step seriously. The initial description of your business that you present in early ads and communications will attract buyer queries, and your personal assurances and explanation will further interest. But it is highly unlikely you will develop purchase intention until you share hard-copy documents presenting provable facts, figures, and financial and operational facts about your business. Be ready when the need arises – and it will!

As you assemble, review, and finalize the records and materials you will need to present during the sale process, use the form titled **Business Sale Documentation Checklist in the Digital Toolkit.** It lists documentation requirements with space for you to indicate whether the document is ready for presentation, whether it needs to be created, or whether it needs to be revised, either to bring it up to date or up to professional presentation standards.

> **Step 2: Key Takeaways**
>
> Necessary financial records and business documents include:
>
> - Professionally produced financial statements, records, and contracts.
> - Facts and records that verify business condition.
> - Confidentiality agreements.
> - Business sale agreements and contracts.
>
> Financial statements should be produced in accordance with generally accepted accounting principles (GAAP) and all documents must accurately represent the conditions of your business.

Step 3: Finalizing Your Asking Price

Chapter 1 helped you answer the question on the mind of all business owners as they begin to think about a business sale: What's my business worth? It helped you arrive at an early estimate of the value of your business and guided you toward improvements that could maximize its attractiveness and worth.

Now, with your business prepared for a sale, it is time to answer the question on every buyer's mind as they think about a business purchase: What is the purchase price?

Doing the Math

The number you arrived at as an early valuation estimate will almost certainly differ from the price you set for your business sale, which will be based on your final, accountant-verified annual earnings, the conditions of your business and the terms of your sale offering, and expert input from your sale advisors.

Based on widely accepted valuation approaches (detailed in Chapter 1), pricing your business will likely involve a formula that multiplies seller's discretionary earnings (SDE) by a number between 1 and 5, using this formula:

Current Annual Earnings
called seller's discretionary earnings (SDE) or adjusted cash flow

x

Multiple of Earnings
usually a number between 1 and 5
that is based on comparable market research
and condition of business strength and attractiveness
adjusted to account for business weaknesses or risks
and further adjusted based on attractiveness of sale terms

=

The Starting Point for Pricing Your Business

The price you arrive at through this multiple-of-earnings calculation will almost certainly be adjusted with input from your business sale advisors.

Once finalized, it will establish the asking price for the tangible and intangible assets of your business – probably not including such assets as cash, accounts payable minus accounts receivable, non-operating assets such as your car, or real estate owned by the business. When structuring the sale, covered in Chapter 6, you will either exclude those assets from the offering or sell them separately.

Making Price Adjustments

To finalize the price of your business, work with your sale advisors to consider the following adjustments:

- Have you accurately judged the attractiveness of your business, and therefore its earnings multiple?
- Will you be providing seller financing by accepting a portion of the business sale price over time and with interest – a condition that supports a higher price and in most sales leads to a higher asking-to-selling price ratio?
- Is your price in line with prices of comparable business sales? Go to bizbuysell.com to access the Valuation Report. It provides recent listing and sale data that will help you benchmark the prices and earnings multiples of for-sale and recently sold businesses similar to yours in terms of industry, location, and

financial performance. The findings will help you compare the prices of comparable businesses, keeping in mind that asking prices and selling prices nearly always differ. (See the Chapter 1 section titled "Market Approach to Valuation" for more information.)
- How much will the asking price be adjusted to account for price negotiations? Most buyers negotiate the asking price and for that reason, most businesses are offered at prices up to 20 percent, though more often 10-15 percent, higher than the price the seller expects to achieve. The aim is to state a price that accommodates the anticipated asking-to-selling price variance without stating a number so high that it reduces buyer interest and inquiries.
- Will the final price be adjusted to include the price of business-owned real estate, if any? Real estate is typically valued and sold separately and not included in the initial business sale price.

As you calculate your selling price, use forms titled **Earnings Multiple Assessment Worksheet and Seller's Discretionary Earnings (SDE) Calculation Worksheet in the Digital Toolkit**. Both are described in Chapter 1 and each includes in-form instructions for entering your business information. The forms calculate results automatically.

Step 3: Key Takeaways

Business pricing steps involve:
- A pricing calculation that multiplies seller's discretionary earnings (SDE) by an earnings multiple, usually between 1 and 5, that accurately reflects business strength and attractiveness.

Pricing adjustments to account for:
- The positive pricing effect of favorable sale terms.
- Comparable-sales valuation research.
- Anticipated downward price negotiations that contribute to higher asking prices.
- The value of real estate and excess inventory or working capital that is being purchased by the buyer.

Step 4: Preparing Your Business Selling Memorandum

Whether you are selling your business on your own or through a broker, you will need to be ready to present a thorough written overview of your business and why it is a good purchase prospect.

Some brokers call this presentation a selling memorandum or selling memo. Others call it a confidential description book or an offering memo.

- If your business is very small and will likely sell for under $200,000, you can probably reduce the selling memorandum to a terms sheet that presents your business description, financial information, asking price and terms.
- If your business is large, and if its assets, products, and systems are detailed and extensive, your selling memorandum will likely run considerably longer to adequately explain your offerings and its price. This may require a selling memo summary, covered later in this chapter.

Selling Memorandum Contents

The selling memorandum includes:

- Facts about what your business is and does and what makes it an attractive purchase opportunity, without revealing sensitive information that you or your ultimate buyer won't want non-buyers (especially competitors) to know.
- Accurate statements that don't stretch the truth or overlook weaknesses, as you'll need to warrant the accuracy of all information you've provided before a sale closes.
- Earnings and asking price information without disclosing financial statements.
- An inspiring presentation that prompts buyers to take the next step in the purchase process.

> *The selling memorandum is the first complete description of your business that your prospective buyer will see. It needs to strike a careful balance between delivering facts and also offering an inspiring description of your business and its future potential.*

It should include the following information, which is described in greater detail in the **Selling Memorandum Checklist in the Digital Toolkit**.

- **Business description**, including business structure, history, products, and financial overview.
- **Business location**, including building description and lease information.
- **Business strengths**, including competitive advantages and forces that could provide growth opportunities.
- **Competitive overview**, including competitive position and advantages.
- **Products and services**, including descriptions, distinguishing features, and sales trends.
- **Operations**, including operating hours, seasonality, equipment, inventory, processes, and staffing.
- **Marketing**, including an overview of the industry, geographic area, competitive overview and trends, and a summary of the marketing approach, plan, and opportunities.
- **Staffing**, including an overview of key employee titles, job descriptions, length of employment, compensation, credentials, and contracts (without revealing names).
- **Growth projections**, including descriptions of growth opportunities accompanied by estimates of time, financial resources, and staff required.
- **Potential buyer concerns**, including issues a buyer might see

as a purchase barrier, accompanied by descriptions of current or planned actions that ease or overcome the concerns.
- **Financial information**, including a statement of whether the business uses an accrual or cash-basis accounting method and a one-line summary describing seller's discretionary earnings (without including financial statements).
- **Offering price and terms**, including asking price, contents of sale, sale payment terms, buyer qualifications, if any, seller's timeframe, and statements regarding seller's willingness to remain during a transition period and to sign a non-compete agreement.
- **Appendix**, including supporting information described in the **Selling Memorandum Content Checklist in the Digital Toolkit**.

The **Selling Memorandum Content Checklist** will be a useful guide as you customize your contents and keep your assembly effort on track.

Sharing Your Business Information – Confidentially

Before divulging business information, work with your broker or advisors to establish a plan for how to respond to inquiries generated by your business-for-sale ads. Consider the following approach:

- Create a selling memo summary. Especially if your selling memorandum runs many pages long, your selling memo summary will become your initial response to inquiries generated by your business-for-sale ads, though only after confidentiality agreements have been signed and received.

The selling memo summary should include the following information:

- Business name and owner's name, with contact information. This information will be deleted prior to distribution and will not be revealed until prospects have been screened, determined to be serious and financially capable, and have signed confidentiality agreements.
- Business description, exactly as presented in the selling

memorandum.
- A business overview of strengths, competitive position, financial performance.
- Offering price and terms, as in the selling memorandum.

By sending only the summary as a first response to inquiries, you allow yourself time to further assess the buyer's interest and financial capability before divulging the full contents of your Selling Memorandum.

Before releasing your selling memorandum, be ready to require the prospective buyer's confidentiality and non-disclosure agreements, using a form provided by your broker or attorney. For an example, see the **Mutual Confidentiality Agreement Sample Template in the Digital Toolkit.**

Buyers understand they need to agree to maintain confidentiality, so be ready with the form and don't hesitate to ask for a signature and legal commitment.

Step 4: Key Takeaways

Sale presentation materials include:
- A selling memorandum with a confidential, accurate, inspiring description of your business and why it's a good purchase prospect, including earnings and asking price information, without disclosing sensitive information or financial statements. For very small businesses, the selling memorandum can be replaced with a terms sheet that presents business description, financial information, asking price, and terms.
- A selling memo summary for use as an initial response to inquiries.

Be prepared to present and require agreement to a confidentiality agreement before releasing the selling memorandum, with its complete description of your business, to the buyer.

Key Terms

Buyer's Personal Financial Statement: A form requested by the seller to verify the buyer's financial capability to make the business purchase.

Comparable-Sales Valuation: A value estimate made by comparing the size and strength of a business to recent sales or asking prices of similarly sized businesses in the same business sector or market area. Also called a market-comparable valuation.

Earnings Multiple: A number, usually between 1 and 5, but sometimes higher for large or very profitable businesses, that reflects the profitability and projected future strength of the business.

GAAP: Generally accepted accounting principles, the preferred format of professionally produced financial statements.

Confidentiality Agreement: A legal document signed by two or more parties who agree not to reveal sensitive information obtained during private discussions; a necessary form to obtain before identifying the business name to a prospective buyer. Further, a non-disclosure agreement (NDA) requires that proprietary information remain private. If signed by both the seller and the buyer, it is called a Mutual Confidentiality Agreement.

Offer-to-Purchase Agreement: A legal document that itemizes the price, assets, terms, and conditions involved in the sale and clarifies the rights, obligations, and responsibilities of the buyer and the seller.

Seller's Discretionary Earnings (SDE): The amount a business generates annually for the benefit of its owner and a key figure of interest to business buyers. SDE differs from business profit by adding back deductions for owner salary, insurance, auto use, memberships, and other benefits; discretionary expenses another owner may choose not to make; expenses for non-recurring purchases; and deductions for interest, taxes, depreciation, and amortization. Also called annual earnings or owner's cash flow.

Seller Financing: A sale payment approach that allows the business buyer to pay a portion the purchase price when the sale closes, and to pay the remainder of the price, plus interest, over a specified period, usually backed by security and other agreements.

Seller Financing Note: A legal document required by sellers who plan to accept a portion of the business sale price over time and with interest, a condition that enhances most sale offerings and leads to higher asking-to-closing prices.

Selling Memo Summary: A document for use in initial responses to prescreened and prequalified inquiries, but only after receipt of the required confidentiality agreement. The summary presents a business description and business overview including strengths, competitive position, financial performance, offering price, and terms. It also includes business and owner name and contact information, although that information is initially withheld.

Selling Memorandum: The first complete document describing the business and the sale offer that the prospective buyer will see. It presents facts about the business and what makes it an attractive purchase opportunity, without revealing sensitive information that the owner or the ultimate buyer would not want others, and particularly competitors, to know.

Digital Toolkit Resources

Access the digital toolkit by visiting https://www.bizbuysell.com/seller/guide/selling-a-business/.

Broker Interview Notes
Mutual Confidentiality Agreement Sample Template
Business Sale Documentation Checklist
Sales and Profit Growth Chart
SDE Calculation Worksheet
Earnings Multiple Assessment Worksheet
Selling Memorandum Checklist

5

Marketing Your Business for Sale

At this point, you have met with the team of professionals who will advise you through the sale process, you have assembled all the necessary documentation, and you have determined a fair asking price. Everything is buttoned up and ready to go. Now it is time to let prospective buyers know your business is available for purchase.

Marketing your business for sale, while keeping it confidential, is not only necessary but also possible. You just have to strike the right balance between getting the word out to your targeted audience of prospective buyers without letting word of your sale leak to those whose confidence in your business could be shaken by the news.

This chapter covers the steps to follow, including:
- Protecting confidentiality.
- Options for marketing your business for sale.
- Creating an effective business-for-sale listing.
- Managing your listing and the inquiries you receive.

Most owners choose to keep plans for a sale to themselves, their advisors and only a few confidents. The following sections help you sort through and decide on your options.

Step 1: Maintaining Confidentiality

Announcing your business for sale isn't an occasion for guerrilla marketing. Unless you are reaching out to a prospective person or business you believe is likely to buy your business, all marketing of your business needs to be presented in a manner that conceals your personal and business identity.

You don't want to risk tipping off customers, creditors, competitors, or employees, whose concern could weaken your business at the very time you want to keep it in its best condition.

- **Have a confidentiality agreement ready for presentation** to serious, qualified prospective buyers. The **Mutual Confidentiality Agreement Sample Template in the Digital Toolkit** presents an example of the details to cover. This necessary agreement can be provided by your broker, prepared by your attorney, or obtained through a legal form shop or website. In any case, be sure your attorney reviews the form and that it includes a clause that ensures mutual confidentiality, along with an expiration date that allows the confidentiality assurance to expire after a designated term.

- **Establish a private email account** for use exclusively when communicating with prospective buyers and business sale team members. Select an address that reveals neither your name nor your business name, for example landscapingoffer@, or even a lineup of random letters and numbers.

- **Direct phone calls to a nonbusiness number.** Avoid using your personal phone number, as employees and others may quickly recognize it, and others can use a reverse phone number lookup to learn the name and address associated with the number. When calls come through, be prepared to answer in person or with a voicemail message that conveys appropriate greetings without revealing your name or the name of your business.

- **Wait for a signed letter of intent to purchase** before sharing proprietary processes, trade secrets, client lists, or financial details about your business. Your sale listing likely displayed annual revenues and owner's cash flow, along with asking price. <u>Do not share further financial details, even with a signed confidentiality agreement, until the prospective buyer has demonstrated clear intent and ability to purchase.</u>

- **Be prepared for questions from employees and associates** who may suspect your sale intention. You can be truthful without announcing your plan. You can say you are developing an exit plan to ensure ongoing stability for your business. Or you can say you're talking to potential partners or successors, without stating you will be leaving the business near-term.

- **Be aware that while confidentiality is essential in most business sales**, there are exceptions, such as in the following situations, where confidentiality could hinder the sale effort. Use your judgment regarding whether such scenarios such as these apply to your situation:
  - A business located in a rural market that operates as the only business in a certain category.
  - A well-known and respected business in a local market area that would benefit from widespread knowledge that the brand is for sale.
  - A fire-sale scenario, for example an owner has suddenly died, and the business is no longer operating.
  - A sale to employees, a partner, or a family member.

> **Step 1: Key Takeaways**
>
> Be prepared to maintain confidentiality:
>
> - Be ready to present serious, qualified prospective buyers with a confidentiality agreement.
> - Establish a private email account and phone number for use exclusively with prospective buyers, both to conceal your personal and business identity until you're ready to disclose it and to avoid tipping off employees (and others) and causing concern within your business.
>
> Don't share proprietary processes, trade secrets, client lists, or financial details about your business until you have a signed letter of intent to purchase.

Step 2: Defining Your Likely Buyer

Deciding how and where to present your business to prospective buyers involves decisions about who is most likely to consider your business for acquisition.

- Is your likely buyer seeking to buy a business specifically like yours? Buyers considering businesses within specific business sectors are most likely reached through industry-specific listings, industry-specific brokers, and online business-for-sale sites.
- Is your likely buyer seeking to buy any business rather than a business specifically like yours? Buyers considering a wide range of businesses are most likely reached through brokers and online business-for-sale sites.
- Is your likely buyer seeking to buy a business specifically in your geographic location? Buyers who live or want to live in the region where your business is located, and who are considering a wide range of business offerings specifically in your geographic area, are most likely reached through local market listings, local brokers, and online business-for-sale sites.

- Is your likely buyer an investor or an investor group seeking to acquire a business of your type in several geographic locations? Investors and investor groups seeking business such as yours are most likely reached through industry-specific listings, industry-specific brokers, and confidential inquiries.
- Is your likely buyer a competitor or supplier of your business? A competitor or supplier is best reached through a confidential inquiry.
- Is your likely buyer an individual who seeks a business of your type and who must have specific credentials, certificates, or licenses to acquire your business? Buyers with specific professional credentials are best reached through industry-specific brokers, online business-for-sale sites, and confidential inquiries.
- Is your likely buyer seeking to acquire a franchised business? If you are selling a franchise, known as a franchise resale, consult with your franchisor before beginning the sale process. Franchise sales involve contractual obligations. Also, the franchisor may have a list of interested buyers to share with you. If not, online business-for-sale sites will help you reach the broadest range of prospective buyers.

When both the buyer and seller come from the same geographic area, the sale is a local-market transaction, which describes the majority of all small business sales. Often these deals include a local broker and, almost always, they involve online business-for-sale searches. Just as people search online for real estate in their own market areas, they also search online sites for businesses for sale in their community.

Targeting Advertising Efforts Only to Those Likely to Buy Your Business

If you are working with a broker, the marketing of your business becomes the broker's responsibility. If you will not have a broker on your sale team, the responsibility will be yours.

Step 2 helped you clarify the profile of your likely buyer and where that buyer is most likely looking for businesses like yours. That information puts you in the best position to create your marketing plan or to evaluate the plan your broker recommends.

- **Buyers seeking businesses only in specific market areas** often work through professional contacts or through online searches. Online searches usually lead to online listing sites, where buyers filter results to show only listings for businesses in the desired market area. Professional contacts lead to local business brokers, bankers, accountants, attorneys, or business leaders. You can provide these individuals with advance information about your sale intentions by making discreet contacts, often working through your confidential attorney or accountant relationships.

- **Buyers seeking businesses only in specific industries or professional arenas** read ads in trade association publications and on websites. They search for opportunities by filtering online listing sites by business type, size, and location. Many also seek leads by networking with industry or professional area association executives, which you can cultivate in advance by making confidential contacts.

- **Nearly all buyers seek businesses through online listing sites.** Whether they are working with a broker, looking for businesses in specific regions or business arenas, or open to a wide range of business and geographic areas, nine out of 10 prospective buyers shop online listing sites.

Online sites are also a rich resource for sellers, who can compare business prices and view the listings of similar businesses to see how they are being presented to buyers.

5: Marketing Your Business for Sale

> **Step 2: Key Takeaways**
>
> Target marketing efforts to reach likely buyers:
>
> - Buyers seeking businesses in specific market areas work through local brokers, read local classified ads, filter online listing sites searching for listings by market, and request leads from bankers, accountants, attorneys, or business leaders.
> - Buyers seeking businesses in specific industries or professional arenas read ads in trade association publications and on sites, and they network with industry or professional association executives seeking leads. Also, they filter online listing sites by business type, size, and location.
> - Nearly all prospective buyers shop online listings, regardless of whether they're working with a broker, seeking businesses in specific locations or business sectors, or open to a wide range of businesses and geographic areas.

Step 3: Creating Business-for-Sale Listings That Attract and Prequalify Buyers

The best for-sale listings are created to attract responses primarily from those who are the most serious and the most qualified to make the purchase. Although it may seem counterintuitive to create listings intended to limit responses, by targeting listings to draw responses only from self-qualified prospects, you protect your time and business information by responding to only the most valid inquiries. Refer to the **Business-for-Sale Listing Worksheet in the Digital Toolkit** for advice on what to include. Access the digital toolkit by visiting https://www.bizbuysell.com/seller/guide/selling-a-business/.

Whether you are writing your listing or relying on the expertise of your broker, here is what it needs to accomplish:

- Entice prospective buyers with attractive facts about the current condition and future potential of your business without even slightly stretching facts, which you will have to warrant as accurate before closing the sale.

- Tell enough about your business to cause buyers to want to know more, but not so much that readers – including competitors – can link the description to your business.
- Indicate your business size and price so it appeals to self-qualified buyers seeking businesses like yours while also allowing those who don't match up financially to rule themselves out.
- Make your business offering stand out among other business-for-sale listings, whether online, in classified ads, or in trade publications.

Providing a Concise Yet Thorough Business Description

You have only a few sentences in which to introduce your business and why it is an attractive purchase opportunity. Every word matters. Your description needs to be clear, compelling, and above all, completely true and accurate.

Here is what your listing needs to convey:

- **What your business is and does.** Get specific with attention-getting facts. Instead of "manufacturing business" say, "manufacturer of low-tech product for high-tech industry". Instead of "marketing firm" say, "a top Florida marketing firm serving national and international clients and winning industry awards for the past seven years."
- **Where your business is located.** If your business is in a major metropolitan market, name the city. If it's in a small town with few similar businesses, instead of divulging your location and possibly your business as a result, you could say, "located in Ohio" or, "located in a vibrant Ohio college town," or some other descriptor that attracts without risking your identity.

An important fact to remember is that many buyers search by location, such as "restaurants for sale in Los Angeles." If you exclude your location, it is likely they won't see your listing.

- **Age of your business.** Buyers want to know if your business is established. Convey the answer in your description, "profitable 12-year-old jazz bar" or in your statement of strengths, "serving government and commercial contracts since 2014."
- **Strengths of your business.** This includes information about its financial strength, products, services, clientele, and other attributes that make it an attractive purchase prospect. Make your strengths part of your description with terms such as "profitable and growing," "consistently strong earnings," "well-known and highly regarded business name," "loyal staff and clients," "high-traffic website and social media presence," "good growth potential." Just be careful that every adjective and every statement can withstand scrutiny both during the due diligence process and as you warrant accuracy when signing a purchase offer.
- **Your asking price.** Most business sale advisors, though not all, advise sellers to include prices in their listings. Although your price might scare some buyers away, the consensus, by a wide margin, is that the advantages outweigh disadvantages. Most buyers looking online for business opportunities shop within price categories. If your price is not listed, your business will not appear in their search results. Also, without seeing your price buyers cannot self-qualify, resulting in inquiries from those without the financial capability to complete a deal of your size. Be aware that while common advice is to state your business asking price, an exception may apply to larger businesses that expect a bidding war. Often, such businesses only disclose earnings, so as not to anchor or limit the sale price.
- **Why you're selling.** This statement is not a have-to-have but if the reason is understandable (retirement, for example) it can inspire trust and increase response rates. Other reasons (burned out, for example) are better left unsaid.

Brokers and sale advisors approach listings differently, but all agree on one point: The description must be brief and specific. It needs to present not a full description but a profile of the business that is capable of catching attention and allowing a buyer to self-qualify interest and ability to make a purchase. It needs to compress facts and strengths into a short description that makes a buyer want to reach out for more. Some intrigue is good. Just be absolutely certain that every word is true.

Concealing Your Business Identity

Using a broker relieves many confidentiality concerns because the broker will market the business, receive inquiries, and handle responses. If you're marketing directly, protect your business identity with this advice:

- **Place what are called blind ads** that do not reveal your business name or location and that describe your business attributes while camouflaging facts that buyers, competitors, and others can link specifically to your business. Avoid photos that reveal identity.
- **In offline ads, direct responses to a media-provided PO box or email address.** This allows you to conceal your name and business identity. It also allows you to follow up with only the inquiries that seem to come from serious prospects who are qualified to buy and own your business, and to pass on all others.
- **Business-for-sale listing sites use identity-concealing call-to-action features.** Interested buyers are directed to "complete the Contact Form." After you receive inquiries, you can ask questions to determine if they are serious prospects. Before sharing any information about the business, you can then ask them to complete and submit a confidentiality agreement.

The BizBuySell "Ten Commandments" for Online Listings

1. **Include key financials.** This includes annual revenue and annual cash flow or seller's discretionary earnings.
2. **Provide geographic information.** You have the option to

include your location, such as state, county, city, and address, or to keep geographic information confidential. Be aware that most buyers search at least to the county level. If you exclude this geographic information your business is eliminated from the related search results.

3. **Write an attention-grabbing headline.** In any listing, most people read only the headline. If those few words grab their interest, they read more. To draw them in, use keywords they might use during their search. Also, consider which aspects of your business prospective buyers are most apt to find compelling, whether it is your great location, desirable products and services, strong brand and well-known name, clientele, or other factors. Ask yourself this question: What would make you want to buy your business? Write a headline that conveys your answer.

4. **Be easy to contact and prompt to respond.** Direct inquiries to your broker's phone number or, if you aren't using a broker, to a phone number or email address in no way connected to your personal or business name. For a higher level of confidentiality, place blind ads that present no personal contact information, instead funneling responses through media or site-provided contact channels. Once an inquiry from a seemingly well-qualified prospective buyer arrives, be ready to respond quickly and to begin communications detailed in Chapter 6.

5. **BizBuySell allows you to list your business under two categories.** You have the option of listing your business under a "best matching business type" and a "next-best matching business type." Even though a business might at first seem to fit within one category, it is best to select a second category to maximize exposure as long as the second category is relevant. For example, a service station could select "gas stations/service stations" as a best-match business type and extend reach with a second placement under "auto service/repair."

6. **Be descriptive.** Highlight what makes your business unique, its strengths and its potential – with no meaningless details.

Be honest and don't exaggerate. Keep language professional and with no hint of desperation. No OBO (or best offer). No all-caps headlines. No flashy sales pitches such as "Hot Deal. Won't Last Long."

7. **Include photos.** Make your listing stand out with eye-catching photos of your physical location or of your business interior, equipment, or other confidence-inspiring images. Be careful to select images that do not reveal distinguishing features that clients, employees, or competitors could see and then identify your business. At a minimum, include a stock photo that represents your business offering and quality. Whether you shoot your own images or use stock photos, make sure all are clear, uncluttered, non-pixilated, professional-looking and, in the case of stock photos, legally available to use without watermarks.

8. **Balance details with confidentiality.** To keep sale plans from getting out, in all presentations avoid unique details that reveal your business identity. Instead, describe strengths with nonspecific language, for example "one of the leaders in its industry," "established online presence," "located in popular shopping mall along major interstate."

9. **Upgrade your listing if necessary to gain exposure and more leads.** Especially if your business faces high competition, is of high value, is of interest to a narrow buyer segment, is on a short sale timeline, or if you want greater exposure, consider upgrading to a higher listing level. The higher the listing level, the higher your listing will appear in search results, plus you will have the advantage of other features that elevate exposure above basic listings.

10. **Proofread your listing before publishing.** Check for spelling and grammar, for missing words or numbers, and to be sure that the listing communicates clearly and presents your business in a compelling and professional manner. A good practice is to draft your listing in a word-processing app, using spelling and grammar check. Even then, proofread several times. When you

5: Marketing Your Business for Sale

are sure it addresses all ten commandments on this list, you are ready to start marketing.

Requesting Information That Allows You to Prescreen Buyers

- In your listing description, you do not have to state, "Contact the seller for more information." Instead, you can request and require specific information that helps you prescreen and sort respondents by the likelihood they can and may buy your business before inviting personal contact.
- If you are using a broker, that person will prescreen responses on your behalf.
- If you are placing your own ads in offline media, you can make this requirement part of your first email response. Your instructions might read, "Thank you for your inquiry about my business. Please reply with a description of your business background, the type and size business you seek to acquire, when you plan to purchase a business, your investment capabilities, and your interest in this business."

Serious buyers will understand your efforts and will reply with the requested information.

> ### Step 3: Key Takeaways
> Create listings that attract and prequalify buyers:
> - Buyers want to know what your business is and does, where it is located, when it was founded, business strengths or attributes, financial trends, asking price, and why you are selling.
> - Tell enough to attract buyers and cause them to want to know more but not so much that readers – including competitors – can link the description to your business.
> - Indicate your business size and price to attract buyers seeking businesses like yours and to help those who do not match up financially to rule themselves out.
> - Be concise. Be truthful. Balance details with confidentiality. Proofread carefully.

Step 4: Managing Your Listing and the Inquiries You Receive

Your listings have now been written and placed.

Your selling memorandum should be ready to share with serious and qualified prospects (if not, turn back to Chapter 4).

You should have obtained a signed confidentiality agreement before releasing your sale information.

Now it is time to track which listing channels are performing best and to manage the inquiries your listings generate.

Tracking Responses

If you advertised your business in a number of outlets – newspaper classified ads, online sites, and an industry-specific newsletter, for example – keep track of which responses, and especially which well-qualified responses, come from which ad placements. This information will guide decisions as you make adjustments, if necessary.

- **If the wording in some listings pulls more and better-qualified inquiries than the wording in others**, the finding will help you revise non-performing listings to better match the content of strong-performing listings. An advantage of online listings and classified ads is that both can be almost immediately updated. Do not hesitate to make revisions as you feel necessary, and do not hesitate to read broker and online listings for inspiration.
- **If your listings in various outlets are all the same or similar**, study which outlets delivered the highest number and most-qualified inquiries. You can use that finding to shift marketing efforts toward the best-performing sites or publications.

As you track your marketing efforts, don't get impatient. The average business takes 6-12 months to sell. During the marketing phase, your listing tracking stats will be valuable in guiding your decisions.

Screening, Prioritizing and Initiating Communication with Buyers

As you respond to inquiries generated by your listings, begin with this dose of reality: Most sale advisors will tell you that nine out of ten respondents never make a purchase. A good many lack the qualifications or financial capabilities. Others are "just looking."

- **Some are wannabe shoppers** who would like to buy a business but are in no way ready to make a purchase.
- **Some are tire-kickers** who are simply curious about the kind of opportunities they might pursue.
- **Some are competitors** masquerading as buyers in order to gather intelligence.
- **Some are what the industry calls "sharks,"** searching for sellers who appear overly anxious and may be ready to accept rock-bottom prices.

Your job, or the job of your broker if you are using one, is to separate strong respondents from all others, which involves these steps:

1. Be clear about the qualifications the person who buys your business must possess. What business experience, professional certifications, or other factors are absolutely required? How much cash must the buyer be able to provide on closing day — either as a full payoff or as a sizable down payment? If you are offering a seller financed loan, what type and size of collateral will you require as security? What timeframe must the buyer be prepared to act within?
2. Screen and sort respondents based on their ability to meet your necessary qualifications. Your listings will provide information that helps unqualified buyers opt themselves out. Once you receive inquiries, your buyer requirements will help you assess each respondent's capabilities before pursuing their interest further.

BizBuySell Guide to SELLING YOUR BUSINESS

Inquiries from buyers who appear to be fully qualified will become your strong prospects, but first you will need to verify their facts. If you are working with a broker, that person will handle this task. If you are working on your own, you will want to involve your attorney and accountant as you request copies of bank statements, financial statements, professional licenses and certificates, and other documentation.

Qualified and serious prospects will be prepared for such requests. Often, however, they will feel comfortable releasing information only after signing mutual non-disclosure or confidentiality agreements and only as part of a trust-building quid pro quo exchange during which you release facts and financial information about your business in exchange. At this point, you will be launching the sale process – the topic of Chapter 6.

As you review each inquiry generated by your for-sale listing, use the **Buyer Inquiry Prescreening Checklist in the Digital Toolkit**. It lists qualification-assessment questions with room for your evaluation: Yes, No, or Maybe.

Access the digital toolkit by visiting https://www.bizbuysell.com/seller/guide/selling-a-business/. Inquiries accompanied by a line-up of yes answers become your hottest prospects. Complete one form for each inquiry to make later reference easier.

5: Marketing Your Business for Sale

> **Step 4: Key Takeaways**
>
> Track and prescreen respondents:
>
> - Track inquiry response rates to determine which listings placed in which media outlets or on which listing websites pull more responses than others. Revise wording and investments based on the findings.
> - Separate respondents who appear to match the qualifications you seek in a buyer. Request, through your broker if you are using one, information to verify facts about their qualifications before releasing facts and financial information about your business – a step covered Chapter 6.
> - In online listings, request that respondents provide their purchase timeframe, business experience and financial capability. In print ads, present the request for this necessary information in your immediate reply to ad responses. When using a broker, that person will handle prescreening on your behalf.
> - Prioritize listing respondents based their ability to meet your financial timeframe and experience requirements. Those who match up will become your strong buyer prospects – the ones with whom you will promptly begin communications and negotiations, the topic of Chapter 6.

Key Terms

Blind Ad: An ad in which the identity of the seller or the business is not revealed. Responses are directed to a media-provided address, a broker, or to a private email account or phone number established to conceal personal and business identity and for use exclusively with prospective buyers.

Confidentiality Agreement: A legal document signed by two or more parties who agree not to reveal sensitive information obtained during private discussions; a necessary form to obtain before identifying the business name to a prospective buyer. Further, a non-disclosure agreement (NDA) requires that proprietary information remain private. If signed by both the seller and the buyer, it is called a Mutual Confidentiality Agreement.

Franchise Resale: The term for the sale of an existing franchise. Franchise resales begin by consulting the franchisor, who will have mandated steps to follow and who may have a list of interested buyers to share.

Intramarket Transaction: A business sale that involves a buyer and seller who are in the same geographic area, which describes the majority of all small business sales.

Online Business-for-Sale Sites: Websites where sellers and brokers post listings to reach buyer prospects who begin their searches online. The largest online sites are bizbuysell.com and bizquest.com

Warranties and Representations: A statement in a buyer's purchase offer and contract that requires the seller to warrant or guarantee that the business is in the condition as represented and that facts as presented are accurate to the best of the seller's knowledge. From the first ad to the day of closing, sellers must share information that is absolutely accurate. Should a buyer learn otherwise, the sale can be jeopardized, and the buyer can seek recourse.

Digital Toolkit Resources

Access the digital toolkit by visiting https://www.bizbuysell.com/seller/guide/selling-a-business/.

Mutual Confidentiality Agreement Sample Template
Business-for-Sale Listing Worksheet
Buyer Inquiry Prescreening Checklist

6

Navigating the Selling Process

Your business is now officially on the market.

You have received inquiries and put any that appear to have the professional ability and financial means to purchase your business on your list for rapid response. Next up is to prepare for the face-to-face meetings and negotiations in front of you, while also managing additional inquires as they arrive.

Your broker, if you are working with one, will guide you through the selling process ahead.

This chapter outlines the steps involved, from prioritizing prospective buyers based on their qualifications through to the moment you accept a buyer's offer:

- Verifying prospect qualifications.
- Meeting prospective buyers and establishing trust.
- Preparing for questions buyers will ask.
- The pros and cons of seller financing.
- Negotiating and accepting a buyer/seller friendly offer.

Step 1: Verifying Qualifications and Prioritizing Prospects for Follow-Up

In your listings, or in your initial reply to inquiries, you requested information to answer your first qualifying questions about prospective buyers:

- Do they possess the necessary experience, education, certifications, or licenses?
- Does their purchase timeframe match with yours?
- Are they seeking a business like yours and of similar size and price?
- Are they financially capable of buying your business and can they meet your closing day financial expectations?

Based on the facts, you can quickly sort respondents into cold-, warm-, or hot-prospect categories.

Requesting Additional Information if Necessary

An advantage of listings that don't identify you or your business is that you will not have to respond to all inquiries. Most cold prospects will be set aside, possibly permanently, but a few may be worth later follow-up.

- **If respondents didn't submit the required information**, you have two choices. You can move the inquiry to your "cold-prospect" column, feeling that the lack of information tells you what you need to know: either they cannot or chose not to provide the answers, or they are sleuthing rather than seriously shopping. However, if based on the incomplete information you have received you think the person may be adequately qualified, reach out for more information.

    Without providing your business or personal name, reach out and ask again for the qualifying information. Your message might read, "Thank you for your interest in my business and sale offering. I look forward to providing more information.

First, would you please reply with information about the size of business you are looking to acquire, your cash investment plans, and your ability to back a loan, if one is necessary, with collateral security?"

Even after receiving the required information from prospects who appear qualified, you may choose to research independently, online or through discreet inquires, before following up.

- **Especially if the prospect is a competitor**, or a person who works for a competitor, begin by getting a mutual confidentiality agreement and, even then, request the buyer's personal and business background information before sharing further information about your business. This will test the prospect's level of interest. Only those serious about purchasing will be willing to reveal their own financial information.
- **If most inquiries seem to lack necessary experience or financial capability to buy your business**, reconsider the wording in your listings. Rework your business description and call-to-action to help buyers better understand your business, price, and financial requirements and to help them self-qualify before responding.

Step 1: Key Takeaways

Verify prospect qualifications:
- Require prospects to accompany responses to your listings with information about their business experience, certifications or licenses, purchase timeframe, the type and size of business they are seeking, and their financial capability.
- Request and require additional information, if necessary.
- Do not reveal your name or your business name until you receive a signed confidentiality agreement.

Step 2: Quickly Reaching and Beginning Discussions with Qualified Prospects

As soon as a prospect appears uniquely qualified, financially capable, and a good match with your business, issue an immediate response.

If you are working with a broker, that person will handle the follow-up on your behalf.

- **Pick up the phone.** Identify yourself if your name is not likely to reveal your business identity. Otherwise, explain that you are the owner of the business they inquired about.
    - Convey your thanks for the inquiry and your preliminary belief in the buyer's suitability with your offer.
    - Use the conversation to confirm your impression about the person's qualifications and capabilities. Without revealing your business identity, develop rapport through a discussion that provides and obtains information in an answer-to-answer trade-off. For example, to learn more about the buyer's cash condition, offer some financial information first. You could roughly describe your business size before explaining that the sale requires $X cash down at closing. This gives the buyer some information before requesting financial information in return.
    - *Expect as many as half of respondents to drop out at this point* because they lack the financial capability or the business experience to continue discussions. Better to learn this now than later.
- **Email your selling memo summary.** If you believe the prospect is an able and likely buyer, share your selling memo summary (see Chapter 4), but only after deleting all identifying

information. Do not share your full selling memorandum at this point.
- **Schedule a first meeting.** To keep your business identity concealed, choose a location outside of your business; the office of your accountant or attorney is a good alternative.
  - If a confidentiality agreement hasn't already been obtained, explain in advance that you will begin the meeting by presenting such an agreement, after which you will be able to share specific facts about your business.
  - Explain that the prospect's accountant or attorney is welcome to attend this meeting. Simply by attending the meeting, the prospect conveys a high level of interest. Bringing legal or accounting advisors adds further demonstration of intent.
  - If geographic distance makes an on-site meeting improbable, set up a phone or video meeting to be attended by you, your accountant or attorney, and the prospective buyer and accompanying advisors. Prior to the meeting, exchange confidentiality agreements.
  - During the meeting, refer to the selling memo summary you previously provided (without business identification). Discuss your business description and overview, using the discussion to reassess buyer interest and deepen confidence in the buyer's intent.
  - Restate the offering price and terms as presented in the selling memo, summarizing the purchase structure in terms of the buyer's required cash investment at closing and the need for solid security if you are offering a seller-financed loan.
  - If the meeting reconfirms your assessment of the buyer's interest and ability, be prepared to move onto the next step. Otherwise, end discussions at this point, expressing thanks for the interest while explaining that the buyer's situation and your expectations appear not to match up.
- **If you have only obtained a confidentiality agreement** from

the prospective buyer, at this point also obtain a non-disclosure agreement (NDA). The **Mutual Confidentiality Agreement Sample Template in the Digital Toolkit** includes agreements to both confidentiality, which requires the buyer to keep confidential information secret, and non-disclosure, which forbids the unauthorized disclosure of all sensitive information. If the prospective buyer does not pledge confidentiality and non-disclosure, end discussions at this point.

- **Share your selling memorandum.** With confidence in the prospect's intent and financial ability to purchase your business, and after obtaining a signed confidentiality and non-disclosure agreement, share but don't yet release your selling memorandum. Give the buyer time to review it carefully but do not allow the prospect to take it from the meeting until you are very confident of the likelihood this person can and will buy your business.
  - When you are ready to release the selling memorandum, <u>number the cover sheet and have the prospect initial every page</u>. Should you learn that copies of pages end up in the wrong hands, you can trace their origin.
  - If the prospect indicates reduced interest or you have reduced confidence, probe, address and overcome concerns – or end discussions at this point.
- **Tour and present your business.** Schedule the visit when your business is in prime physical condition and during a time when it is active and impressive. If yours is a very small business and a tour may spark staff questions, be prepared to introduce the prospect as a colleague, associate, or friend, or consider an after-hours tour.

Describe and point out features of your business and its strengths and opportunities. Conduct the same kind of tour you would provide to industry or community VIPs, showing how a customer experiences your business before going behind the scenes to provide an overview of how your business works and produces its products or services. Do not reveal trade secrets, proprietary processes, or information that should be kept from anyone but the ultimate buyer of your business.

Encourage and answer questions, learning more about and addressing the prospect's abilities and concerns. If you have concerns or the prospect indicates reduced interest that cannot be overcome, end discussions at this point.

- **Immediately following the tour, hold a private meeting to address the prospect's questions.** Be prepared to answer the questions outlined in the next section of this chapter. Take care not to reveal insider or highly confidential information. Also, do not negotiate your asking price at this point. If the prospect indicates reduced interest or concerns that cannot be overcome, end discussions at this point.

- **Use the post-tour meeting to learn more about the prospect.** Inquire about past business ownership, desired purchase timeline, and how long their search for a business has been going on. Ask how the prospect plans to fund a purchase, and who else will be involved in the purchase decision (for instance, a spouse, partner, banker, attorney). If the answers cause you uncertainty about interest or capability, address and overcome concerns or end discussions at this point.

- **Provide requested information.** The next formal step in the buying process is for the prospect to hand you, or your broker, a letter of intent to buy your business. To keep interest moving toward that point, provide requested information such as marketing materials, product samples, or other information that heightens interest without divulging confidential business workings. If you sense the prospect has lost interest or lacks the ability to pay the price required (which, after negotiations, may end up at 10-15 percent below your asking price), address and overcome issues or end discussions.

> **Step 2: Key Takeaways**
>
> Quickly reach qualified prospects:
>
> - Make personal contact. Schedule a first meeting outside of your business or via phone or video if necessary, without revealing business identity.
> - Require a signed non-disclosure agreement before releasing your selling memorandum to a person you are very confident will become your buyer.
> - Tour and present your business without identifying the prospect as a possible buyer and without revealing trade secrets, proprietary processes, or insider information.
> - Meet to further confirm interest and capability and to answer the prospect's questions but not to negotiate your asking price at this time.

Step 3: Preparing for Questions Buyers Are Likely to Ask

Your buyer will want to confirm the following facts about your business:

- That it delivers immediate cash flow.
- That it is a going concern with an established infrastructure.
- That it is in strong financial condition backed by good historical data and financial statements.
- That it has a broad-based, loyal, and transferable client base and workforce.
- That operations can be transferred to and assumed by a new owner with few or no transition hiccups.

Your selling memorandum should present the facts that deliver these assurances. Beyond that, however, be prepared for the following questions.

Why Are You Selling?

What do you plan to do after the sale? If you do not have a clear and ready answer, the buyer can jump to the wrong conclusion and think your business is in distress and you want out. In truth, most businesses sell because the owners are either burned out or tired. Even that truth can be presented positively, with a statement such as, "After 15 years the business is in great shape, and it is time for me to turn it over to a new owner with fresh energy and ideas to take it to the next level."

If your sale is prompted, at least in part, by the fact the business is struggling, focus on its prospects and why you want to place it in the hands of someone with the energy and talent to pursue the opportunities in the turnaround or repositioning plans that you will share with the new owner.

How Much Do You Earn from the Business Annually?

Money is a major factor in business sale decisions. Most buyers seek businesses that assure a great job and income for the owner, along with a good return on investment.

The best way to answer the "how much does it earn" question is with verifiable facts presented in your seller's discretionary earnings (SDE) statement, which should be included in your selling memorandum. If you have not already created this statement, turn back to Chapter 1 for an explanation and use the **SDE Calculation Worksheet in the Digital Toolkit** to enter required numbers and calculate your earnings.

As a quick refresher, seller's discretionary earnings, also called SDE, annual earnings or owner's cash flow, differ from annual business profit on your income statement, which deducts all possible expenses to arrive at the lowest-possible taxable income.

Seller's discretionary earnings reflect the amount of potential earnings available to the business owner based on the company's normalized earnings and owner salary.

Working from the business income statement, the calculation adds back deductions for owner salary, auto use, memberships, and other personal and non-business related expenses. It also adds back discretionary expenses another owner may not make, expenses for non-recurring purchases, and expenses for interest, depreciation, taxes, and amortization.

The result is how much the owner earns annually from the business. This is the number buyers want to see. If they are looking at several businesses, it is the number they will use as a basis for comparison.

Is Your Asking Price Reasonable?

Be ready to share your pricing rationale. If your business has been professionally appraised, share the report summary. Also share:

- How you arrived at the earnings multiple used in initial pricing, which includes assessments of the strength and attractiveness of your business.
- How your sale price compares to prices of similar businesses in your market area and industry or business sector.
- The value of tangible assets. This allows the buyer to see that a portion of the price is backed by physical fixtures, furnishing, and equipment.
- The value of intangible assets. This gives you the opportunity, again, to present the value you place on your workforce, loyal clientele, business operations and processes, intellectual property, brand name, marketplace and online presence, and brand reputation.

Address the pricing question with a good explanation, and see

How Much Has Your Business Grown Over Recent Years and What Do You See for Its Future?

> *Buyers know that past performance is a good indicator of future prospects. Be prepared to share facts.*

Be ready to present the following:

- Recent sales and earnings, which can be presented in a graph that charts the past 3-5 years of financial trends. Enter your numbers in the **Sales and Profit Growth Chart in the Digital Toolkit**. Access the digital toolkit by visiting https://www.bizbuysell.com/seller/guide/selling-a-business/. It will automatically create a graph for presentation. If your business experienced any down years, be ready to describe circumstances and how they were addressed.
- Number of customers added over recent years, including information on customer loyalty and customer descriptions.
- Number of staff added, perhaps accompanied by a description of improvements in earnings per employee over recent years.
- Operational or equipment improvements that have enhanced efficiency and effectiveness, and increased production and profitability.
- Price increases that have been favorably accepted.

Also share other growth indicators, such as expanded facilities, improved ratings by industry evaluators, positive customer reviews, favorable publicity, and other facts that demonstrate increased business strength.

BizBuySell Guide to Selling Your Business

Is the Business Likely to Transfer Easily and Run Successfully After the Sale?

Transferability is a major concern to buyers, who want assurance that passing the business from one owner to another will be smooth if not seamless.

Be prepared to address the following transferability concerns:

- **Is the business location secure?** Especially if your location is key to success, your buyer will want to know the lease is secure for at least the next 3-5 years. In advance of the sale, negotiate a lease extension, if necessary. If you own the building, be prepared with supporting documentation to describe prospective lease arrangements. If your business is fully or partially conducted online, describe how your website and other accounts are owned and ready for transfer.
- **Are operations easy to transfer?** Be ready to discuss business and marketing plans, operations and employment policy manuals, and other materials that document the workings of your business. Do not release the documents, as the prospect may or may not be the buyer of your business but offer assurance that they will be transferred to the new owner following the closing of the sale.
- **Will staff remain loyal to the business?** Most buyers want to hear that one or a few top staff members with knowledge of operations and customers will remain with the business after the sale. Be prepared to discuss transferable employee contracts and non-compete agreements, if any, as further assurance.
- **Will customers remain loyal to the business?** If customer loyalty is key to business success, get client lists in order before

the sale. Buyers feel more assured if they see there are a large number of customers rather than a few, and that many have long-standing relationships with the business – the largest with contracts or agreements that will transfer with business ownership. Also, expect questions about whether customers are loyal to the business or to you, personally, in which case a longer transition period may offer assurance that there is time for relationship handoff.

- **Are you willing to stay with the business during a post-sale period?** Willingness to remain with the business during a post-sale period, usually 3-12 months, gives the buyer confidence and supports a higher selling price. Unless the business is in strong condition and very easy to transfer to a new owner, the seller's desire for a rapid departure can lead to doubts and lower selling prices, especially if the seller also requests all-cash payoff at closing.

Are There Business Risks to Be Aware Of?

Anticipate this question well in advance of the sale and take preemptive action to reduce or eliminate risks before presenting your business for sale. To a buyer, the big red flags to avoid include:

- Low or declining sales and earnings.
- No key staff member who will stay on after the sale.
- Lack of documents detailing how the business runs.
- Unprofessional financial records.
- Dependency on only a few clients, or clients who are loyal to the owner rather than the business and its offerings.
- A declining industry or market area.
- Lack of documents detailing how the business runs.
- A problematic, nontransferable, or soon-to-expire building lease.

If risks are few, you can discuss any turnaround efforts you have already outlined and present them as growth opportunities. Better, though, to overcome as many weaknesses in advance as possible, keeping areas of concerns to only a few, if any.

Are You Open to Payment Terms?

Payment terms can make a positive difference in your asking price and in the final negotiated price a buyer pays. Sellers willing to take a good portion of the sale price at closing and the remainder through a seller-financed loan attract a larger buyer pool. Also, seller financing contributes to higher asking prices and, after buyer negotiations, higher asking-to-closing prices than sales requiring all cash at closing.

Though you will negotiate and finalize pricing and payment terms as you structure and finalize the sale prior to closing, early on be ready to address this key question. The next section describes payment approaches and facts to consider.

Step 3: Key Takeaways

Be prepared for questions buyers ask:

- Why are you selling?
- How much do you make from the business annually?
- Is your asking price reasonable?
- How much has your business grown over recent years and what do you see for its future?
- Will the business transition and run successfully after the sale?
- Is the business location secure?
- Are operations easy to transfer?
- Will staff and customers remain loyal to the business?
- Are you willing to remain with the business during a post-sale transition period?
- Are there business risks to be aware of?
- Are you open to payment terms?

Step 4: Determining Your Business Sale Payment Approach

Very few business sales involve a full cash payoff at closing.

The vast majority of business sales involve small businesses, and the vast majority of small business buyers reach into their savings accounts, sell stock if they own any, borrow against their home equity, use their retirement funds, or enlist help from family members – and then pay the rest of the price with a loan.

The few buyers that deliver cash payoffs on closing day offer the cleanest, quickest sale exit. They also, however, deliver a tax burden to the seller, who receives payment of the full business price at the time of the sale, significantly increasing the owner's annual income and income taxes.

Other payment approaches include:

- **Third-party financing.** This payment approach most often involves a loan provided by a bank or credit union. For all but highly qualified loan applicants purchasing very low-risk businesses, third-party financing can be complicated and time-consuming. If part of the buyer's payment will come from a third-party loan, early in discussions request a prequalification letter from the lender to avoid time-consuming delays later.

  Most third-party loans take one of three forms:
  - **Traditional business loans** can provide favorable terms and interest rates, but usually they also have strict qualification requirements including that the loan applicant have strong business experience and a high credit rating, and that the business being purchased has substantial tangible assets.
  - **SBA 7(a) loans** are offered by SBA-certified banks, microlenders, and commercial lenders and are guaranteed by the SBA in case of loan default. To qualify, an applicant must have a personal credit score that exceeds the SBA required minimum, adequate business experience, and assets to commit as collateral. Also, they must be purchasing a

business with a written business plan and annual earnings that exceed a required minimum level. SBA loans involve red tape and time and serve only a small percentage of sole proprietorships.
- **Home-equity loans** require buyers to use the equity in their home as collateral on a loan that is usually limited to a percentage of the home's fair market value, minus any outstanding loan obligations. A home-equity loan is secured by the home, so no payments can be missed, and the home cannot be used to secure any other loans.
- **Stock exchange.** This payment approach applies only when a business is being acquired by a corporation and paid for with stock, usually publicly traded stock, rather than with cash. This payment approach applies to very few business purchases, but should it become a possibility for your business, consult your attorney and accountant to weigh the obligations and risks involved.
- **Seller financing,** also called a seller-financed loan, involves a loan much like any other, but the seller, rather than a bank, is the lender. In most small business sales, the seller finances a portion of the purchase price by agreeing to accept a closing-day payment followed by payments from the buyer over time and with interest following the terms outlined in a promissory note.

The Pros and Cons of Seller Financing

More than nine out of ten small business sales and nearly half of mid-sized business sales involve seller financing.

The Advantages of Seller Financing

- Buyers view seller financing as a favorable payment term that enhances their attraction to the business offering, reduces price negotiation, and results in higher asking-to-closing prices than sales requiring an all-cash payoff at closing.
- A seller's willingness to accept deferred payments heightens

the buyer's confidence in the seller's assessment of the future prospects of the business.
- Seller financing leads to a faster sale closing by eliminating the time-consuming need for bank or SBA loan applications and approval.
- By eliminating the buyer's need for loan-origination or other fees, seller financing provides the seller with a negotiating advantage when other price concessions are requested.
- The seller receives tax advantages due to the fact that income from a seller-financed loan is spread over years rather than delivered in a single year, which can place the seller in a higher tax bracket.
- In addition to receiving a payoff over time, the seller also receives interest income over the duration of the seller-financed loan.

Seller Financing Risks and How to Minimize Them

The first risk to an owner offering seller financing is that a buyer can default on payment obligations.

The second risk is that a buyer can deplete the resources – the inventory, condition, or goodwill of the business – and then default on the loan. Even if your loan conditions allow you to foreclose and take your business back, by the time of default its condition may be far below its closing-day value.

The biggest reason for default is a buyer who turns out to be a poor business or financial manager. Take preemptive action with three essential steps:

- **Verify the buyer's qualifications** from the very first inquiry up to the moment you agree to finance a loan. Request financial and business background information, then require copies of tax returns, bank statements, credit reports, and references. Then do further research on the buyer's background and reputation, online and within your industry or business sector.
- **Obtain a promissory note**, also called a loan note or note payable. It includes:

The name of the promisor, the person who is promising to fulfill the obligations of the loan.

The name of the promisee (also called the obligee or payee), who is accepting the promise outlined in the note.

The principal amount, which is the amount being loaned under the terms of the note.

The interest rate, which is usually close to but often a little but not much higher than bank loan rates at the time.

Repayment terms, which include the interest rate and payment due dates.

A default clause that makes the entire outstanding balance of the loan due if a payment is missed within a certain number of days of the established due date.

CAUTION: Free legal advice sites provide samples of promissory notes, but because laws vary by state, and because this is such an important document, do not proceed without advice from your legal advisor.

- **Protect yourself further by obtaining a secured promissory note.** The promissory note secures the buyer's promise to repay you following the terms of the agreement. It does not, however, secure the note or provide you with recourse if the buyer fails to make payments or declares bankruptcy, at which time all secured creditors would be paid first.

  A secured promissory note gives the lender, in this case you, the legal right to collateral should your buyer not make the payments as promised.

- **Require collateral to secure the loan.** Collateral can take several forms, including business assets, a personal guarantee, or a third-party guarantee. Each form of collateral comes with risks to avoid.

  - **Accepting business assets as loan security** basically gives you the right to take back the business in the event of default. *The risk is this:* If the buyer has taken on other lenders, those lenders may have first rights to assets, and you would have a

6: Navigating the Selling Process

subordinated position with access only to remaining assets after others are paid. Further, the buyer may have depleted inventory or even sold valuable assets before finally defaulting on your loan.

For these reasons, lenders in seller-financed loans require collateral beyond business assets alone.

- **Accepting a personal guarantee as loan security** basically gives you the right to pursue personal assets.

   The risk is this: If you sold your business as a corporation or LLC, the loan agreement would have been between your corporation (called OLDCO during the sale process) and your buyer's newly established business entity (referred to as NEWCO). For that reason, the person to whom you sold the business no longer owns it, but rather his or her NEWCO does.

   Even if you sold the business to the buyer and not to a NEWCO, sometime after the sale the buyer may have transferred business assets into a corporation or limited liability corporation (LLC), of which your buyer is now a shareholder rather than the owner of the assets you sold.

   For these reasons, lenders in seller-financed loans need to obtain the buyer's personal guarantee (and also the buyer's spouse's personal guarantee if your attorney so advises). This allows you to pursue personal and jointly owned assets, if necessary.

   CAUTION: Securing a seller-financed loan requires legal assistance. In some states it takes the form of a cognovit note that paves the way to rapid judgement and loan collection.

- **Accepting a third-party guarantee as loan security** provides assurance that a high net worth relative or associate will guarantee the debt. Before accepting this option, do your homework. Require the guarantor's financial statement and credit report and take all other steps detailed in the due diligence section of Chapter 7.

Step 5: Receiving and Accepting a Buyer/Seller Friendly Offer

The end isn't yet in sight but you are nearing the finish line.

At this point, you have nearly completed six of the seven chapters of this book and all the steps that lead to the culminating moment when you receive the buyer's offer.

- You have readied and priced your business.
- You have screened initial responses to your sale offering and followed up with seemingly capable prospects.
- You have verified the qualifications of your prospects and narrowed your candidates to those who best fit with your business and exit plan.
- You have determined your most qualified buyer prospect and provided information about your business.
- You have answered questions and shared your objectives for sale timing and payment.
- You have verified your trust in the buyer's qualifications to buy your business.

It is now time for your top buyer prospect to make a move.

This is the moment when you, or your broker, receives a letter of intent to buy your business.

Receiving the Buyer's Letter of Intent

The letter of intent outlines the buyer's purchase proposal. Be sure that, either directly or through your broker, you receive this offer in writing. If it comes in the form of a conversation, do not begin discussions. Instead, ask the buyer to detail price and terms in writing so you can respond thoughtfully with input from your accountant and attorney.

The letter of intent is not a binding legal document, but it forms the basis for all following discussions that lead, if all goes well, to the formal purchase offer.

The letter of intent outlines:

- **The buyer's proposed purchase price.** This price will likely be lower than the one to be settled on during negotiations, as buyers expect the first offer to be countered, so they rarely put the maximum price they are willing to pay into the purchase proposal.
- **The proposed purchase structure.** The structure will likely include the amount to be provided as cash-at-closing and the amount to service as debt.
- **Terms and purchase conditions.** Among other conditions, this part of the letter of intent states that the offer is contingent on issues to be addressed before the sale closes.

The form of the letter of intent varies, and the responsibility for its preparation is with the buyer, and not with you. You will, however, need to be prepared to review it carefully, and then to respond following the information in the next section.

As you and your sale team members study and plan your response to the proposal you have received, use the form titled **Letter of Intent Checklist in the Digital Toolkit**. It defines each component of the buyer's proposal, as well as the ramifications and adjustments you will want to consider.

Responding to the Buyer's Proposal

Based on advice from your sale advisors, you will accept the buyer's offer or, if your primary requirements differ, you will propose a counteroffer.

Be aware that this is not the time to negotiate fine points. Your objective is to reach agreement on the major elements of the proposal, including price, payment structure, exclusions or additions to the sale, timeframe, and your after-sale involvement.

Agreeing on other sale details will happen during the negotiations of final terms that will take place prior to drawing up the final purchase agreement and closing the deal – all covered in Chapter 7.

BizBuySell Guide to Selling Your Business

Accepting the Buyer's Offer

To accept the buyer's offer, you and the buyer will sign either the initial letter of intent or a version that reflects mutually agreed-upon changes. Either way, once your signatures are on the line, the letter signifies agreement to a purchase offer. Here is what typically happens next:

- **Your broker, if you are using one, will collect a deposit**, usually 10 percent of the proposed purchase price, to be held in an escrow account.
- **If you are not using a broker**, you and your sale advisors will decide whether to require a deposit, called earnest money, from the buyer. If earnest money is involved, once collected it is held in a third-party escrow account until any conditions stipulated in the letter of intent are adequately addressed and the sale closes.

From this point, the sale moves into the due diligence stage.

More work and more negotiation lie ahead. But take a deep breath, and realize you have successfully attracted and accepted an offer from a qualified buyer.

Congratulations!

Step 5: Key Takeaways

Receiving and accepting the buyer's purchase proposal:

- The buyer will present a letter of intent directly or through your broker. It will present the proposed price, purchase structure, terms, and purchase conditions. If it comes in the form of a conversation, request the offer in writing.
- After consulting with your sale advisors, sign to accept or propose a counteroffer to the major points: price, payment structure, exclusions or additions to the sale, timeframe, and your after-sale involvement.
- Upon reaching agreement, sign the initial letter or one reflecting agreed-upon changes. Your broker will then collect a deposit to be held in an escrow account. If you are not using a broker, you may decide to require an earnest money deposit to be held in a third-party escrow account until the sale closes.

Key Terms

Collateral: Assets pledged as security for repayment of a loan, to be forfeited in the event of a default. Real estate and assets of the business being acquired are common items pledged as collateral in seller-financed loans. Additionally, because the loan recipient's home equity might be otherwise pledged as collateral for other loans, and because the value of business assets could be depleted by the time of loan default, most owners also require other forms of loan security, typically in the form of personal guarantees from the buyer and the buyer's spouse and possibly from a third party.

Earnings Multiple: A number, usually between 1 and 5 but sometimes higher, that reflects the profitability and projected future strength of the business, and which forms the basis for arriving at the business asking price.

Letter of Intent: A non-binding written document that presents a prospective buyer's proposed purchase price, purchase structure, and purchase terms and conditions. Whether accepted as is or after the seller's counteroffer, it forms the basis for discussions and negotiations that lead to a formal purchase offer.

Non-Disclosure Agreement (NDA): A legal contract that establishes a confidential relationship between those signing the agreement, who agree that sensitive information they may obtain will not be revealed to others.

Promissory Note: Also called a loan note or note payable, usually created between individuals rather than institutions. It includes the name of the *promisor* who is promising to fulfill the obligations of the loan; the *promisee* who is accepting the promise as outlined in the agreement; the principal amount being loaned under the terms of the note; the *repayment terms*, including the interest rate and payment due dates; and a default clause that makes the outstanding balance due if a payment is missed within a certain number of days of the established due date.

Secured Promissory Note: A secured promissory note gives the lender the legal right to seize designated collateral should the loan recipient fail to make loan payments as promised. While a promissory note secures the loan recipient's promise to repay the loan following the terms of the agreement, a secured promissory note provides recourse in the event of default or bankruptcy.

SBA 7(a) Loan: A loan offered by SBA-certified banks, microlenders, and commercial lenders and guaranteed by the Small Business Administration (SBA) in case of loan default. To qualify, an applicant must have a personal credit score that exceeds the SBA required minimum, adequate business experience, and assets to commit as collateral, and must be purchasing a business that meets qualification requirements.

Seller Financing: A sale payment approach that allows the business buyer to pay a portion of the purchase price when the sale closes, and to pay the remainder of the price, plus interest, to the seller over a specified period, usually backed by security and other agreements.

Seller's Discretionary Earnings (SDE): The amount a business generates annually for the benefit of its owner and a key figure of interest to business buyers. SDE differs from business profit by adding back deductions for owner salary, insurance, auto use, memberships, and other benefits; discretionary expenses another owner may choose not to make; expenses for non-recurring purchases; and deductions for interest, taxes, depreciation, and amortization. Also called annual earnings or owner's cash flow.

Selling Memo Summary: A document for use in initial responses to prescreened and prequalified inquiries, but only after receipt of a signed confidentiality agreement. The summary presents a business description, business overview including strengths, competitive position, and financial performance, offering price, and terms. It also includes business and owner name and contact information, although that information is initially withheld.

Selling Memorandum: The first complete document describing the business and the sale offer that the prospective buyer will see. It presents facts about the business and what makes it an attractive purchase opportunity, without revealing sensitive information that the owner or the ultimate buyer would not want others, and particularly competitors, to know.

Digital Toolkit Resources

Access the digital toolkit by visiting https://www.bizbuysell.com/seller/guide/selling-a-business/.

Letter of Intent Checklist
SDE Calculation Worksheet
Sales and Profit Growth Chart

BizBuySell Guide to Selling Your Business

7

Closing the Sale and Transferring the Business

You and the buyer have agreed to the buyer's purchase proposal, and you're holding a signed letter of intent to purchase your business. You've come a long way since your first decision to sell.

You are nearing the finish line, but don't take your business listing off the market. Not yet.

Still in front of you are all the steps involved with due diligence, sale agreements, the closing process, and, finally, transferring the business to its new owner.

This chapter guides you through the steps:
- Preparing for and conducting due diligence.
- Agreeing upon the sale structure.
- Negotiating final sale terms.
- Understanding the purchase and sale agreement.
- Preparing for the closing process.

- Closing the sale.
- Passing the baton.

Step 1: Performing Due Diligence

An easy definition of due diligence is "serious investigation."

At this point, you have agreed to the buyer's letter of intent to purchase, although the price, terms, and conditions of the proposal are contingent on verification, which happens during the period of due diligence.

In almost all sales, due diligence is a condition of the buyer's offer. Only after determining that business conditions meet expectations, or that problem conditions have or will be satisfactorily addressed, will the buyer remove the due diligence contingency in the purchase proposal. And only then can the sale closing begin.

During due diligence, the buyer examines in detail the financial condition, business operations, and any legal issues of your business. Your role, as the seller, is twofold:

- Be prepared to provide access to all the information the buyer will want to examine.
- Be ready to simultaneously examine the buyer's financial condition and managerial experience, especially if you will be carrying a seller-financed loan or agreeing to accept deferred payments for a portion of the purchase price.

Assembling the Necessary Documentation

The buyer, and the buyer's accountant and attorney, will need to inspect the financial records and operations of your business.

By now the buyer should have signed confidentiality and non-disclosure agreements. The buyer's letter of intent to purchase most likely stated that the offer was contingent upon a due diligence investigation. Agreement to due diligence is almost always accompanied by a statement that prevents either party from

7: Closing the Sale and Transferring the Business

disclosing confidential information obtained during the investigation to anyone other than the buyer's or seller's purchase advisors.

Even with signed agreements assuring confidentiality, however, do not release the documents. Instead, present them only in a setting you establish for due diligence review.

Be prepared with the following long and essential list of required documents:

- **Federal tax returns** for the past three years, allowing the buyer to verify the revenues shown on financial statements. If your business is a C corporation, present corporate tax returns. If your business is a sole proprietorship, LLC, or S corporation that passes revenue through to you personally, present Schedule C of your personal return.
- **Business income statements and balance sheets** for the current and the past 2-3 years, plus a current cash flow statement, all presented as professionally reviewed reports following industry standards.
- **Statement of seller's discretionary earnings or owner's cash flow**, presenting how much money the business generates annually for the benefit of its owner.
- **Financial trends and ratios**, including revenue and profit growth trends.
- **Accounts receivables/accounts payable lists.**
- **Inventory list**, including value.
- **Major equipment and furnishings list**, including value.
- **Supporting financial information**, such as inventory turnover rate, receivable collection rate, and current or liquidity ratio.
- **Current building lease**, including lease duration and transferability.
- **Fixtures, furnishings, and equipment list**, including all items included in the sale with photos of major items, titles confirming ownership, lease and maintenance agreements, and depreciation schedules from the most recent tax return.

- **Copies of contracts and agreements** with employees, customers, suppliers, distributors, and others.
- **Intellectual property documentation** for patents, trademarks, and other items, each showing ownership by the business rather than by individuals.
- **Management and operational documentation**, including procedure manuals, product and price lists, other reports, and agreements.
- **Staffing records**, including a description of employee benefits plan, organization chart, employee policy manual, and a list of employees with hire dates, salaries, contracts, and benefit summaries.
- **Client information**, including relationship descriptions and agreements.
- **Supplier and distributor lists**, including relationship descriptions and agreements.
- **Business and marketing plans** or summary descriptions.
- **Current business licenses, certifications, or registrations**, including verification of transferability.
- **Business formation documents.**

To assist in assembly of necessary documents, print and use the **Due Diligence Documentation Checklist in the Digital Toolkit.** Access the digital toolkit by visiting https://www.bizbuysell.com/seller/guide/selling-a-business/.

Balancing Confidentiality with the Buyer's Need for Business Examination

During due diligence, the buyer will want to meet staff, business clients, and suppliers, but you will not yet be ready to make your sale public. The following approaches can help you manage interactions.

- **Consider revealing sale intentions to a very few key managers** if you and the buyer will need their help during the business examination. Seek an agreement with the buyer that

these top-level employees will be offered bonus compensation for assisting in the sale process and transition. When informing these select staff members, stress the buyer's strong qualifications and positive plans for the future of the business. Also, convey the due diligence timeline and the importance of keeping the sale confidential during that period.
- **Reduce the buyer's presence in your own business setting** by relying on your broker, if you are using one, or your accountant. Their offices can serve as a repository for the documents the buyer needs to access. They can also provide the setting for meetings with you and key staff members.
- **Keep interactions with the buyer private.** Confirm with the buyer how to contact you, likely through the email address and phone number you established specifically for sale purposes. While initially those contact approaches were to conceal your personal name and your business name, at this point they can keep the buyer's interactions less visible to staff members and others.

Preparing for the Scope of the Buyer's Investigation

Plan to devote significant time to prepare for and assist with the buyer's investigation. Plan also to invest in the services of your accountant and attorney, who will help you determine what information to divulge and how to protect confidentiality if, and most likely when, the buyer requests to share sensitive information with third-party advisors.

The buyer's due diligence will likely focus on an examination of three aspects of your business:

- **Financial condition**, looking beyond previously provided financial statements to assess financial management and growth potential.
- **Business operations**, including production and other processes and how easily they will transfer to a new owner, the nature

and transferability of clients or customers, billing and collection procedures, banking relationships, details about staffing and management, and current business and marketing plans.
- **Legal issues**, including information on legal obligations or potential legal problems ranging from pending litigation, pension liabilities, claims, tax audits, zoning issues, and a wide range of other possible issues that your attorney can help you list and prepare to discuss.

Investigating the Buyer's Capabilities

Due diligence is not just for buyers. Especially if you are accepting part of the purchase price through seller financing, due diligence provides you another opportunity to verify the ability of the buyer.

Whether you are providing a loan or other form of deferred payment, examine the ability of the buyer both to make payments and to run your business in a manner that ensures its success.

- **Obtain the buyer's personal financial statement and credit report.** Work through your broker or obtain this information on your own. Then ask your accountant to review the information, examining the buyer's financial strength.
- **Conduct an online search for the buyer's name** to view online mentions, posts, and publicity that might reveal facts the buyer has not shared. Additionally, search for the buyer's name along with the names of businesses the buyer was previously associated with to learn more about the buyer's business history.
- **Request and contact personal, financial, and business references** in an effort to determine whether the buyer presents a management or loan risk. If you and the buyer have decided not to reveal purchase intentions until after the sale, confirm with the buyer how to introduce yourself. For example, you could tell the reference you are conducting reference checks regarding a top-level position in your business.
- **Interview the buyer regarding plans to significantly alter**

your business, perhaps by changing its location, product line, pricing, or staffing. This information will help you determine whether the buyer's plans are consistent with assurances you may have recently given to key staff and customers. Also, the information will help you assess whether you believe the business is likely to succeed after such changes, and therefore whether it is likely to generate the earnings necessary to make any deferred payments you are agreeing to accept. (Chapter 6 includes specific information on how to protect yourself when self-financing part of the purchase price.)

Be Patient

Due diligence investigations can easily take a month or longer, especially if the sale involves difficult-to-evaluate assets or if it will be structured as an equity sale that involves the transfer of stock – and therefore the transfer of all known and unknown liabilities of the business. (The difference between asset sales and equity sales is defined in the next step in this chapter.)

The buyer's letter of intent likely stated the due diligence timeframe – normally a month or longer – so you will go into it knowing roughly what to expect. What you may not anticipate is how intrusive and tiring it may feel. Remind yourself, repeatedly, if necessary, that this is necessary to get you to the next step – the negotiations that lead to the sale closing and the transfer of your business.

> ### Step 1: Key Takeaways
> Performing due diligence:
> - Present all documents the buyer will need to examine when assessing the financial condition, business operations, and any legal issues facing your business.
> - Protect confidentiality during the buyer's due diligence. Involve very few key managers. Hold documents and meetings off-site. Keep buyer-seller interactions private by using an email account and phone number established specifically for sale purposes. Involve your accountant and attorney as you determine what information to divulge and how to respond when the buyer requests to share sensitive information with third-party advisors.
> - Conduct seller due diligence by examining the buyer's capabilities, especially if providing seller financing or accepting deferred payments for part of the purchase price. Obtain the buyer's personal financial statement and credit report. Conduct online research. Request and contact personal, financial, and business references. Learn the buyer's post-sale business plans to assess the likelihood of success.
> - Be thorough, diligent, and patient.

Step 2: Structuring the Sale

Once your business and your buyer both pass due diligence successfully, the next step is to finalize the structure of the sale. This involves negotiating and agreeing to four variables:

- What you are selling.
- The price.
- How the price is allocated among IRS asset classes.
- How the price will be paid, which is called the payment structure.

Determining What You Are Selling: An Asset Sale Versus an Entity Sale

There are two kinds of business sales: asset sales and entity sales, which are also called stock sales.

7: Closing the Sale and Transferring the Business

To repeat the comparison offered in Chapter 3, which likens a business sale to a home sale, an asset sale is akin to selling only the contents of the home, while an entity sale is akin to selling the home, including all its assets and all but specifically excluded liabilities. Each form of business sale has distinct advantages for the buyer and the seller, but rarely the same advantages for both.

Asset Sales

In an asset sale, the seller keeps the actual, legal structure of the business, called the business entity, and sells only the tangible and intangible assets of the business, which the buyer moves into a newly formed business entity.

If you are selling a sole proprietorship, without question yours will be an asset sale because sole proprietorships have no stock to sell. The sale of a corporation or LLC, however, can take the form of an asset sale or an entity sale, and so the structure becomes a point of negotiation.

Benefits to a seller in an asset sale include:

- **Nonessential assets can be excluded from the sale**, such as cash, investment accounts, vehicles, equipment, and other assets for which the buyer may not want to pay.

- **Valuable assets can be retained by the seller and leased back to the business.** For example, if a seller owns the building the business is in, the seller might retain the asset, therefore avoiding taxes that would result from its sale – and also generating future income from a lease or lease-purchase agreement with the new business owner.

- **A portion of the purchase price can be allocated to goodwill**, which is treated as a capital gain and taxed at a rate currently substantially lower than the tax on ordinary income.

- **Due diligence is less time consuming or intensive** because the buyer does not need to search for potential liabilities.

Benefits to a buyer in an asset sale include:

- **The buyer purchases only assets and specifically listed liabilities.** Responsibility for any hidden or unanticipated liability that arises after the sale remains with the seller.

- **The buyer can exclude nonproductive or nonessential assets** from the purchase.

- **The buyer does not acquire the depreciation history of the business.** In an asset sale a good portion of the sale is usually allocated to the purchase of equipment, which is acquired at the stepped-up basis – the price at which they were purchased. The buyer, the new owner, can begin depreciating those purchased assets and realizing tax deductions that reduce reported earnings and, therefore, taxes.

Entity Sales

In an entity sale, the owner of a corporation sells its stock – or the owner of an LLC sells its member shares – to a new owner. With the sale of the stock or shares, the buyer acquires all the assets and all the liabilities of the corporation or LLC, except liabilities that are specifically listed as exclusions.

CAUTION: Be aware that while entity sales are taxed at preferential capital gains rates, if the business being sold is a C corporation, it can result in what is called double taxation. First, the business pays tax on gains from the sale. Second, the owner or owners are subject to a second tax when the proceeds are distributed to them, this time as ordinary income. However, if the business is an S corporation, business income passes through directly to shareholders and is taxed only once.

Obtain tax advice well in advance of the sale regarding the possible benefit of converting a C corporation to an S corporation. The conversion comes with a lineup of conditions and complications. The tax benefits are often well worth considering, but do not consider going forward without legal and accounting advice.

7: Closing the Sale and Transferring the Business

Benefits for the seller in an entity sale:

- **Entity sale proceeds are taxed at the capital gains rate**, which is currently considerably lower than proceeds taxed as ordinary income.

- **In an entity sale, liabilities transfer to the buyer** unless they are specifically excluded. This eliminates the seller's risk of responsibility for an unforeseen liability that arises in the future. In an asset sale, responsibility for unforeseen liability remains with the seller.

Benefits for the buyer in an entity sale:

- **In an entity sale, leases and contracts transfer with the sale.** Because contracts, even government contracts, were with the business, they remain with the business as part of the entity sale. In an asset sale, the business is being dissolved and each contract must be transferred to the new owner, sometimes involving renegotiation and, as a result, sometimes less favorable terms.

- **An entity sale delivers the buyer a future tax advantage when and if the business is again sold as an entity.** During a future sale of the business, the difference between what the owner paid to buy the business – the owner's basis in the business – and the amount paid by a new owner, would be taxed as a capital gain rate rather than as ordinary income.

Most buyers prefer asset sales, primarily because in an asset sale the buyer avoids the risk of inheriting hidden liabilities, and also because assets can be quickly depreciated, resulting in lower reported earnings and taxes.

Most sellers prefer entity sales over asset sales, primarily due to tax advantages.

During buyer-seller negotiations that result in agreement to an asset sale, sellers aim to arrive at a price and price allocation that offsets the accompanying tax concessions.

Negotiating the Selling Price

In the letter of intent, you and the buyer agreed to a selling price, but after due diligence and after negotiations leading to an agreement either to an asset sale or entity sale, almost certainly the initially presented price of the business will be adjusted.

Price adjustments will reflect some or all of the following considerations:

- **The higher or lower value placed on business assets** following the due diligence examination.
- **The amount of cash required at closing.** Higher amounts due at closing, up to an all-cash payoff, are often accompanied by the buyer's effort to negotiate a lower price.
- **Items excluded from the purchase.** To accept a lower price, sellers may exclude assets that can be sold separately or leased back to the buyer.
- **The seller's ongoing involvement with the business.** Sometimes, in return for accepting a lower price, a seller agrees to sign and accept future compensation through a management contract. The upside for the buyer is the chance to pay some of the purchase price as a business expense that lowers taxable business earnings. The downside for the seller is that compensation will be taxed as ordinary income. Negotiating employment benefits and perks may offset the negative tax implications.
- **How the purchase price is allocated among IRS asset classes.** A seller might agree to a lower price if a good portion is allocated to asset classes taxed at capital gains rates rather than as ordinary income. The buyer might agree to a higher price if a good portion is allocated to asset classes that result in the fastest possible tax write-offs.

Allocating the Purchase Price

At this point in negotiations, advice from your accountant and your buyer's accountant will be necessary and valuable.

7: Closing the Sale and Transferring the Business

Before closing can take place, you and the buyer must agree on how the purchase price will be allocated among seven IRS asset classes. After the sale, the IRS requires that you both file the identical price allocation using Form 8594, "Asset Aquisition Statement."

- Make purchase price allocation part of your negotiations well before closing day, when the allocation will be included in your closing documents.
- Realize that the IRS requires that the purchase price be allocated among the seven asset classes described in the following section. Also be aware that the IRS can challenge the price allocation, for example by questioning the fair market value of tangible assets or the value placed on intangible assets. For that reason, professional valuations are important for complicated assets.

IRS Asset Classes

The first three asset classes, Class I, II and III, include cash and bank deposits, securities including certificates or deposits, and accounts receivable. Allocations to these categories are not a point of negotiation because they are straightforward to calculate and often not included in the purchase, and therefore have no tax impact.

How the price is allocated to each of the other classes, however, is usually highly preferred by the buyer or highly preferred by the seller, but rarely highly preferred by both, due to tax ramifications. Seek your accountant's advice before negotiating or agreeing to allocations.

- **Class IV - Stock in trade or inventory**, usually valued at original cost or at a defensible fair market value. Buyers often prefer as high an allocation as possible to this asset class, which will qualify as business expenses or for short-term depreciation.
- **Class V - Other tangible property**, including fixtures, furnishings, real estate, vehicles, equipment, and other physical assets, is usually valued at current market replacement value. Buyers prefer a high allocation to physical assets that qualify as business expenses or for short-term depreciation (however, if the buyer must pay sales tax on the assets acquired, the tax may offset the depreciation benefit). Sellers prefer a lower

allocation, unless the tangible property includes appreciated assets that have been held long term and qualify for taxation as capital gains.

- **Class VI – Intangible property.** This asset class covers the value of the operation of the business, including its systems and procedures, intellectual property, customer lists, business books and records, and other assets detailed in IRS Form 8594 instructions. It does not include the value of goodwill or going concern value of the business, which is covered in the next and final asset class.

  These assets are frequently purchased in return for a covenant not to compete – a non-compete agreement – and/or a personal services contract. If payment is made in return for a personal services contract, the buyer can deduct the payment as a business expense, while the seller receives the payment as ordinary income. If payment is made in return for a non-compete agreement, the payment must be amortized over 15 years, making it less attractive to sellers and more attractive to buyers.

- **Class VII – Goodwill and going concern value.** Arriving at the value allocated to this asset class is the result of math and negotiation. The most that can be allocated is the purchase price of the business minus the agreed-upon amounts allocated to the previous six asset classes. The seller will want to allocate as much as possible to goodwill, because the proceeds will likely be taxed as capital gains.

After reading the preceding section, you likely do not need a reminder but it is worth repeating again:

Your accountant is a high-value and necessary resource during allocation negotiations, as well as in the payment structure negotiations that follow.

Agreeing to the Payment Approach

Chapter 6 included a deep dive into the various payment approaches that finance business sales: Third-party financing, SBA 7(a) loans, home equity loans, stock exchanges and – the most common – seller financing in which the buyer makes a closing-day payment, and the seller agrees to accept the remainder over time.

The letter of intent to purchase that you and the buyer agreed upon (see Chapter 6 for information) stated the purchase price, payment structure, and payment conditions of the proposal, including whether the purchase would involve all-cash payoff at closing or, more likely, a closing day payment with the balance paid over future years.

It is now time to structure how the payoff will take place, which involves both negotiation and tax implications.

The two most common options include:

- **Cash down plus a seller-financed note.** As detailed in Chapter 6, the upsides to this approach include tax advantages, as you will spread sale proceeds over several years and avoid the tax impact of a one-time payoff. Plus, you will receive interest income on which you will pay taxes but over the duration of the loan.

   The risk is that the buyer could default, and by that point the business could be devalued of the inventory, physical assets, or going-concern value it had on closing day.

- **Deferred payments through an earn-out.** An earn-out is an agreement that the seller will accept part of the purchase price based on how well the business does in the future. It reduces the buyer's requirement for cash on closing day. It also enhances business attractiveness by demonstrating the seller's faith in the future of the business.

   The risk is that earn-out payments are subject to default if the new owner fails at sustaining the business. Especially if you feel the new owner will grow the business, an earn-out is an attractive payment approach. It provides a negotiating chip that can protect sale pricing while also spreading income over future years and likely providing a tax advantage.

   The earn-out must be defined in the purchase and

sale agreement, including when payments are to be made (typically quarterly, semiannually, or annually), how they are to be calculated, and whether earn-out payments are subject to maximum and minimum amounts, often referred to as caps and ceilings. Most agreements stipulate "calculations must be made by an independent certified public accountant mutually agreeable to the parties."

Step 2: Key Takeaways

Sale structure negotiations revolve around four variables:

- **What you are selling.** *In an entity sale,* the owner of a corporation sells its stock – or the owner of an LLC sells its shares – and the buyer acquires all assets and all but explicitly excluded liabilities of the business. *In an asset sale,* the seller keeps the actual legal structure of the business and sells only the business assets, which the buyer transfers into a new business entity. All sole proprietorships are structured as asset sales. Corporations and LLCs have a choice.
- **The price.** The final price may vary from what was proposed in the letter of intent, based on the value of assets following due diligence examination and the result of negotiations regarding the amount of cash required at closing, the seller's ongoing involvement with the business, and how the price allocation benefits either the buyer or the seller.
- **The price allocation.** The buyer and seller must agree on how the price is allocated across seven IRS asset classes. Your accountant's advice is absolutely necessary. Sellers accept lower prices if a good portion is allocated to asset classes taxed as capital gains. Buyers accept higher prices if a good portion is allocated to asset classes that provide the fastest-possible tax write-offs. The IRS requires the buyer and the seller to file the identical price allocation using Form 8594, "Asset Aquisition Statement."
- **The payment approach.** Few sales include an all-cash payoff at closing. The two most common payment structures are cash down at closing plus a seller-financed loan and cash down at closing with deferred payments through an earn-out agreement based on how the business does in the future.

7: Closing the Sale and Transferring the Business

Step 3: Negotiating Final Terms and the Purchase and Sale Agreement

The end is in sight. What is left before closing are the final decisions regarding sale structure, selling price, asset allocation, and payment structure. Put differently, what is left are the final negotiations.

Preparing for Negotiations

> *Every business sale is different, but nearly all are similar in how buyers and sellers arrive at the closing negotiations: Buyers approach the closing with intent on arriving at the best possible deal before signing the purchase and sale agreement. And sellers intend to do the same.*

Give-and-take negotiation follows. Do not proceed without the following:

- **A signed letter of intent to purchase** that outlines the buyer's proposal and, if necessary, your counterproposal (see Chapter 6).
- **Legal and accounting advice from your broker, if you are using one, and your sale advisors** regarding sale structure, price structure, and a price allocation that provides you the greatest financial benefit at the lowest tax liability.
- **Clarity about your personal financial objectives** including the amount you want to receive at closing and whether you are willing to accept deferred payments through a seller-financed loan and/or earn-out payments.
- **Clarity about issues that must be addressed for the sale to be completed.** Some call these your knock-out factors, deal breakers, or walk-away points. You may have a price figure you are not willing to be below or an amount you absolutely

require at closing. You don't want to be unreasonable, but you do want to enter negotiations knowing the points at which you are willing to say no.

Negotiating Final Agreements

The following list of topics for final negotiation and agreement is included as a **Pre-Closing Negotiation Checklist in the Digital Toolkit**. You will likely refer to it often, celebrating each time you check an item as completed:

- **What is being purchased.** Either you will be selling the assets of your business which will be transferred into a new business entity formed by the buyer (called an asset sale) or your business entity, including all its assets, and all liabilities except those specifically excluded (called an entity sale or stock sale).
- **The purchase price**, which in many cases may be between 10 and 15 percent lower than the asking price. Sellers requiring all-cash payoffs at closing usually settle on prices toward the lower end.
- **How the price will be paid**, including how much will be required as the closing-day payment and how much will be paid through deferred payments.
- **How the price will be allocated** between the seven IRS asset classes.
- **How issues discovered during due diligence will be addressed**, either through price concessions or actions that rectify conditions of concern.
- **How the transition period will be handled**, including how and when the sale announcement will be made; whether employees will be rehired; how and when to contact and notify employees, customers, clients, suppliers, vendors, and distributors; how work in progress will be completed; and how unknown liabilities that become apparent after closing will be addressed.
- **The seller's post-sale involvement with the business**, leading to agreement on the seller's post-sale transition period involvement, timeframe, and compensation, if any; post-sale involvement through a personal services contract, if any; and willingness to

sign a covenant not to compete.
- **Agreement on how contingencies detailed in the letter of agreement to purchase will be addressed or removed.** These include such issues as transfer of leases and contracts and other legal and financial concerns. Also, agreement must be reached on how to address issues that arose during due diligence, whether through price concessions or through actions that rectify the condition.

Use the form **Pre-Closing Negotiation Checklist in the Digital Toolkit**, which defines each topic that must be negotiated and agreed upon prior to closing.

Keep negotiations moving quickly. Pauses will be necessary to obtain input from your sale advisors, but whenever possible limit them to a single day. Delays dampen interest or heighten concern – neither of which supports the kind of healthy negotiations that lead to a successful closing day.

Step 3: Key Takeaways

Final negotiations result in the final terms of your business sale. Before entering negotiations, be prepared with:

- A signed letter of intent to purchase.
- Legal and accounting advice from your attorney, accountant, and broker if you are using one.
- Clarity about your personal price objectives and how much you require on closing day.
- Clarity about the issues you would consider to be deal breakers, whether price, payment, timeframe, ongoing involvement, or other points.

Final negotiations result in pre-closing agreements on the following points:

- Whether the sale is structured as an asset sale or an equity sale.
- Sale price.
- Payment structure.
- Price allocation across IRS classes.
- How issues discovered during due diligence will be addressed.
- How the transition period will be handled.
- How contingencies in the letter of intent will be addressed or removed.

Step 4: Understanding the Purchase and Sale Agreement

At this point in the sale process:

- A buyer has chosen to acquire your business.
- The buyer's in-depth investigation has confirmed the purchase decision, and your own due diligence has confirmed that the buyer has the financial and business capability to complete the purchase.
- You are both ready to reach consensus regarding price, payment structure, price allocation (and the resulting tax implications), and all the other details that comprise the final deal to be detailed in the purchase and sale agreement to be signed on closing day.

Purchase and Sale Agreement Contents

The following list describes the contents of the closing agreement you and the buyer will sign. Behind many of the items lie details that require advice from trained legal experts, which is why your broker and attorney are key partners at this stage.

- **For the simplest sales** – those involving few and uncomplicated assets and a very low selling price – a fill-in-the-blanks "purchase and sale of business agreement" easily found online, will suffice. Before using such forms, however, call on the expertise of your attorney. The agreement you sign needs to comply with the letter of the law in your region, and requirements vary from state to state.
- **For all other sales**, expect the sale agreement to span many pages and to be accompanied by exhibits and attachments that address all the necessary points to be covered. Your broker, if you are using one, will guide you through the process. Otherwise, either your attorney or the buyer's attorney will write the first draft, with the other one reviewing and suggesting amendments – unless you and the buyer agree to both work with and split

7: Closing the Sale and Transferring the Business

the legal fees of a single attorney.

Contents of the purchase and sale agreement include:

- Names of the seller, buyer, and business, including the location of each.
- Assets and liabilities included in and excluded from the sale.
- Closing date.
- Price and how it is allocated across IRS-determined asset classes, along with descriptions of how the price will be adjusted to reflect closing-day valuations.
- Seller agreements of non-competition, management consulting, or post-sale employment.
- Payment terms.
- Security agreements if a portion of the sale will be paid through deferred payments.
- Inventory included in the sale.
- A list of accounts receivable included (or excluded) from the sale and how payments of uncollected receivables will be handled.
- Buyer's and seller's representations and warranties.
- Seller's covenants to transfer the business and its name.
- Employee termination clause confirming how the seller will terminate and pay employees through the termination date and when they may be hired through the buyer's new business.
- The buyer's post-closing rights and obligations.
- Default provisions.
- Business transfer agreements.
- Statements regarding participation or absence of brokers and how buyer and seller will pay professional fees involved with the sale closing.

Refer to the **Purchase and Sale Agreement Checklist in the Digital Toolkit** for details regarding the required items to be covered. Rely on your attorney and your broker, if you're using one, as you review this document, which will become the closing agreement you and your buyer will sign.

> ### Step 4: Key Takeaways
>
> Your broker and attorney are key partners when preparing, reviewing, and negotiating the Purchase and Sale Agreement:
>
> - Only the simplest sales use a purchase and sale of business agreement form found online. Even then, call on the expertise of your attorney. Legal requirements vary from state to state.
> - For all other sales, the agreement is long and detailed. Either your attorney or the buyer's attorney will write the first draft, with the other one reviewing and suggesting amendments – unless you and the buyer agree to both work with and split the legal fees of a single attorney.
>
> The required items to be covered are detailed in the **Purchase and Sale Agreement Checklist in the Digital Toolkit**.

Step 5: The Closing Process

With the sale structure agreed upon, negotiations completed, and the purchase and sale agreement ready to go, it's a race to the finish line.

What awaits is the closing – where the buyer and seller sign pages and pages of documents, the buyer delivers a check for the agreed-upon closing day payment, and all involved take a moment to celebrate before beginning the ownership transfer.

Before you put pens on paper though, you, along with your attorney and your broker, if you are using one, must get all the paperwork in order. The following to-do list is also included in the more-detailed **Closing Paperwork Checklist in the Digital Toolkit**:

- Schedule the closing, preferably on the final day of a quarter, month, or pay period and preferably in the morning so government and bank offices will be open following the closing.
- Agree to the finalized purchase price.
- If the business being sold is a corporation, prepare corporate documents and pass a corporate resolution authorizing the sale.

7: Closing the Sale and Transferring the Business

- Prepare government and tax forms, including those required by your secretary of state or corporations commission; transfer documents for physical assets and intellectual property included in the sale; and fill out IRS Form 8594 showing how the selling price is spread across IRS asset classes.
- Confirm insurance requirements.
- Prepare an itemized list of assets included with and excluded from the sale.
- List and prepare to transfer any work in progress.
- Finalize the list of accounts receivable and accounts payables.
- Prepare loan documents, including promissory notes, security agreements, personal guarantees, and a UCC financing statement to be filed with your state.
- Prepare to transfer your building lease by assembling lease and lease amendments and preparing documents for lease assignment and assignment acceptance.
- Prepare personal agreements for consulting or management agreement and covenant not to compete, if any.
- Prepare exceptions to warranties and representations, if any.
- Prepare succession agreements for employee benefit plans such as profit sharing and flexible spending.
- Prepare the bill of sale that details the terms of the transaction at the time of the sale and makes official the transfer of the business to the new owner.
- Prepare the closing or settlement sheet, which lists the purchase price and all costs and price adjustments to be paid by or credited to the seller and buyer. This will be prepared by your attorney unless your sale is closing though an escrow agent, in which case it will be prepared by the escrow office.
- Prepare the purchase and sale agreement, which in all but the simplest of sales is prepared by the buyer or seller's attorney, with the other attorney reviewing and suggesting amendments, unless the buyer and seller agree to both work with and split the fees of the same attorney. If your broker provides the

agreement, have your attorney review it before signing. It contains descriptions of obligations that are regulated by rules that may vary from state to state.

> **Step 5: Key Takeaways**
>
> To prepare for the closing:
>
> - **Schedule the closing**, preferably in the morning and on the final day of a quarter, month, or pay period, and ensure that all necessary parties can attend.
> - Work with your attorney and your broker, if you are using one, to get all the paperwork listed in the **Closing Paperwork Checklist in the Digital Toolkit** in order.
> - Double check all lists to ensure you are prepared for a smooth closing.

Step 6: Closing the Sale

You have made it to closing day! You are now ready to sign and begin the long-anticipated transfer of your business to its new owner.

If your closing will take place in an escrow office:

- It will follow the instructions provided when the escrow account was opened to hold the buyer's deposit that accompanied the letter of intent to purchase.
- The escrow officer will confirm that all obligations and contingencies in the letter of intent to purchase and in the escrow instructions have been addressed.
- You and the buyer will sign closing documents.
- The escrow officer will transfer funds and record the sale.

If your closing will take place in an attorney's office:

- Your attorney, your buyer's attorney, or both, will prepare and review the purchase and sale agreement.
- Upon legal advice, you will address any outstanding obligations or contingencies.
- You, your buyer, and the attorney who drew up the documents will meet to sign documents and transfer funds.

7: Closing the Sale and Transferring the Business

Whether in an escrow office or attorney's office, the closing day ceremony is an important one.

Here is who will attend:

- The closing will be attended by you and any other owners of the business, along with your spouse and the spouses of other owners (spouses are necessary attendees if you live in a community property state); your buyer or buyers and their spouses (again, spouses are necessary attendees if they live in a community property state); third-party loan guarantors, if any, unless they previously signed personal guarantees or provided powers of attorney to those in attendance; your attorney and possibly your buyer's attorney; your escrow agent (if any); your broker if you are using one; and others whose signature will be required.

Here are the steps you will likely follow:

- **Agree to post-closing final adjustments to the purchase price** to account for prorated expenses and closing valuation of inventory and accounts receivable; usually to be finalized within 15 days of closing.
- **Review and sign the purchase and sale agreement.**
- **Review and sign loan documents.**
- **Review and sign transfer documents**, including lease transfer documents, vehicle ownership-transfer documents, franchise documents, succession documents, and other documents involved in transferring your business or its assets.
- **Review and sign agreements** for the seller's post-closing consulting, employment, and/or non-competition agreement.
- **Review and sign the bill of sale.**
- **Review and sign article of amendment** to change the name of your business, thereby freeing the name for use by the buyer. This step allows the buyer to amend the working name he or she has been using during the purchase process to the name being purchased as part of the sale.
- **Review and sign forms** to transfer patents, trademarks,

copyrights, and other intellectual property assets.
- **Review and agree to the closing or settlement sheet** listing all financial aspects of the sale including how expenses and credits are assigned to each party.
- **Review and agree to the IRS Asset Aquisition Statement**, Form 8594, which you and the buyer must attach to your federal income tax, showing the identical allocation across IRS asset classes.
- **Receive the buyer's payment for the purchase**, either in full or for a sizable down payment, depending on the payment terms negotiated and agreed upon.

And with that, your deal is successfully completed. You did it! You sold your business.

Take time to congratulate yourself and your buyer and to accept congratulations from those around you. Then get ready to make a seamless handoff of your business to its new owner.

Step 6: Key Takeaways

The sale closing will take place in an escrow office or attorney's office.

- **Attendees** include you and any other owners of the business, along with your spouse and the spouses of other owners (spouses are necessary attendees if you live in a community property state); your buyer or buyers and their spouses (again, spouses are necessary attendees if they live in a community property state); third-party loan guarantors, if any, unless they previously signed personal guarantees or provided powers of attorney to those in attendance; your attorney and possibly your buyer's attorney; your escrow agent (if any); your broker if you are using one; and others whose signature will be required.
- The process involves review of, agreement to, and signing of dozens of necessary documents before, finally, the buyer presents payment either for the purchase price in full or for a sizable down payment, depending up the payment terms negotiated and agreed upon.

Upon closing, the sale of your business is now complete.

Step 7: Passing the Baton

What is still in front of you are the lists of details and legal actions necessary to formally transfer your business, to ease its transition to the new owner, and then to begin the transfer into your own new role, whether that means an all-new chapter in your life or an all-new relationship with your business and its new owner.

The following necessary actions await:

1. **Provide the buyer with all information necessary to assume operation of the business, including:**
   - Alarm codes.
   - Computer, software, and online access codes and passwords.
   - Safe combinations.
   - Customer, supplier, utility, vendor, and distributor lists and supporting information.
   - Keys to locks, including building doors, vehicles, and file cabinets.
   - Operating manuals for all equipment.
   - Your personal contact information (if you will not be remaining during a transition period), including where to send all material required by the purchase and sale agreement.

2. **If your business was structured as a corporation or LLC, take legal steps to dissolve your business entity.**
   - Meet with your board, partners, or LLC to pass a resolution to formally dissolve the business.
   - Notify the IRS within 30 days of dissolution, using Form 966.
   - File articles of dissolution with the state where your business was formed and any other state where it is registered. If your business was formed as a sole proprietorship, following the sale it will automatically close once you wind up operations.

3. **Complete forms and actions to cease operations of your business entity.** Rely on legal advice as you complete following

steps:

- Notify contacts for all contracts that are being assigned to or assumed by the buyer.
- Notify creditors to explain how bills will be paid, either by you or the buyer.
- Cancel business permits or licenses, assumed business name, and other registrations.
- Give cancellation notice on your lease if it will not be transferring to the buyer.
- Cancel insurance policies not being assumed by the buyer.
- Pay off bills and collect accounts receivable not being assumed by the buyer.
- Distribute assets remaining in your business after the sale closing, either to yourself if your business is structured as a sole proprietorship or to shareholders, partners, or LLC members.
- Close your employer ID number with the IRS.
- Close business bank accounts and credit cards.
- Close the business line of credit, if any.
- Pay final wages to employees, and pay payroll taxes and fees due to tax authorities.
- File necessary tax forms with advice from your attorney and accountant.

4. **Announce the sale.** There is no longer any reason to keep the news of your sale quiet, although buyers of restaurants or retail shops sometimes shield customers from the news until a transition period is complete and concern over a customer exodus appears unnecessary.

Take the following steps, which are detailed in the checklist titled **Announcing Your Business Sale Checklist in the Digital Toolkit**.

- **Tell your employees.** Begin with key employees before making an announcement to all staff. Opt for a personal presentation by you and the buyer, avoiding email (which

7: Closing the Sale and Transferring the Business

can be quickly forwarded) if at all possible.
- Stress confidentiality until you can contact customers, suppliers, and others.
- Briefly explain why you are selling and your confidence in the new owner's expertise and plans.
- Introduce the new owner who can explain future plans and how employees will transfer to the new organization.
- Share the timeline including when the sale will be made public and why confidentiality is essential until that time.

- **Inform customers, suppliers, and business associates**, reaching out first and personally to those who are most valuable to the business before making a general announcement to all. Move quickly to avoid the news passing through the grapevine.

  If your contact list is long, send all but key contacts an email or regular mail announcement explaining that with great pleasure and after considerable planning you are pleased to introduce the new owner of your business. Share a short statement of why you sold, how long you will remain with the business, if you will, and what you are planning to do next. Include a copy of or link to a complete announcement or attach the news release you will deliver to news outlets.

- **Announce the sale to news outlets.** Prepare a news release or sale fact sheet complete with all facts in a single document that you can distribute to local and industry media, news sites, blogs, and broadcast stations.

  Describe who to contact for more information (and how), when the news can be released, the date of the announcement, a headline summarizing the announcement, and a clear presentation of facts. Consider also including a quote from you or the buyer and a photo of the buyer.

- **Move aside.** Even if you remain with the business during a transition period or thereafter, the business now belongs to its new owner. Help staff, customers, and business associates transfer their confidence by moving yourself out of the

visible leadership role, unless your agreed-upon ongoing role specifies otherwise.
- **Move on.** You have done it! You have sold your business! Now it is time to set a new goal. Chase a new dream. Buy a new business. The choice is yours.

Congratulations!

Step 7: Key Takeaways

After the sale closes, complete all necessary post-closing actions:

1. Transfer all information necessary for the buyer to assume operation of the business.
2. If your business was formed as a sole proprietorship, it will close automatically. If your business was structured as a corporation or LLC, take legal steps to dissolve your business entity. Notify the IRS within 30 days of dissolution and file articles of dissolution with the state where your business was formed and any other state where it is registered. Rely on legal advice as you complete forms and undertake all actions necessary to cease operations of your business entity.
3. Announce the sale. Tell employees, first meeting personally with key employees, if possible, before meeting with or otherwise notifying all employees. Stress the need for confidentiality until the sale is made public.

Share the announcement quickly and personally with key customers, suppliers, and business associates. Then share it with all other business contacts, personally or using email or mail if your contact lists are long, perhaps attaching the news release you will deliver to news outlets.

Distribute the news as a release or sale fact sheet to local and industry media and news sites, blogs, and broadcast stations.

Move aside and help staff, customers, and business associates transfer their confidence to the new owner.

Celebrate!

Key Terms

Covenant Not to Compete: Also called a noncompete agreement. In a business sale, an agreement in which the seller promises not to engage in activities that would compete with the business being sold for a specified period following the date of the agreement.

Due Diligence: In a business sale, the buyer's serious examination of the financial condition, business operations and any current or potential legal issues of the business being purchased, and the seller's serious examination of the buyer's financial condition and managerial experience.

Letter of Intent: A nonbinding written document that presents a prospective buyer's proposed purchase price, purchase structure, and purchase terms and conditions. Whether accepted as is or after the seller's counteroffer, it forms the basis for discussions and negotiations that lead to a formal purchase offer.

Non-Disclosure Agreement (NDA): A legal contract that establishes a confidential relationship between those signing the agreement, who agree that sensitive information they may obtain will not be revealed to others.

Promissory Note: Also called a loan note or note payable, usually created between individuals rather than institutions. It includes the name of the promisor who is promising to fulfill the obligations of the loan, the promisee who is accepting the promise as outlined in the agreement, the principal amount being loaned under the terms of the note, the repayment terms, including the interest rate and payment due dates, and a default clause that makes the outstanding balance due.

Purchase and Sale Agreement: A legally binding document that parties in a transaction use to stipulate the terms and conditions of the sale and transfer of goods or property. In a business sale, the agreement is between the buyer and seller, stipulating what is and is not included in the sale, the selling price and price allocation, and sale provisions and guarantees.

Purchase Price Allocation: How the selling price of a business is allocated across seven IRS asset classes. After the sale, the IRS requires that both the buyer and the seller file the identical price allocation using Form 8594, "Asset Aquisition Statement."

Sale Payment Structure: Few sales are paid in full at closing. The two most common payment structures are cash down at closing plus a seller-financed loan, and cash down at closing with deferred payments through an earn-out agreement.

Digital Toolkit Resources

Access the digital toolkit by visiting https://www.bizbuysell.com/seller/guide/selling-a-business/.

Due Diligence Documentation Checklist
Pre-Closing Negotiation Checklist
Purchase and Sale Agreement Checklist
Closing Paperwork Checklist
Announcing Your Business Sale Checklist

Recommended Resources

American Society of Appraisers (ASA)
https://www.asanorcal.org/

American Institute of Certified Public Accountants (AICPA)
https://www.aicpa.org

America's SBDC
https://americassbdc.org/

BizBuySell Broker Directory
https://www.bizbuysell.com/business-brokers/

BizBuySell Sell Guide Digital Toolkit
https://www.bizbuysell.com/seller/guide/selling-a-business/

BizBuySell Learning Center
https://www.bizbuysell.com/learning-center/

BizBuySell Valuation Report Tool
https://www.bizbuysell.com/business-valuation-report/

International Business Brokers Association (IBBA)
https://www.ibba.org/

M&A Source
https://masource.org/

National Association of Certified Valuators and Analysts (NACVA)
https://www.nacva.com/

BizBuySell Guide to Selling Your Business

Index

A
add back expenses, 9
America's SBDC, 15
announcing the sale, 148–150
annual owner earnings, 9–10
asset sale, 53
asset valuation approach, 4, 5–7

B
BizBuySell Broker Directory, 16
blind ad, 86, 93
build-up rate, 13
business broker, 15–16, 59, 60–62
business condition documentation, 66
business sale documentation, 46, 64–68
business sale team, 58–63
business valuation, 3–17
buyer inquiries:
    managing and screening, 90–92
    qualifying, 96–97
    responding to and meeting, 98–108
buyer's personal financial statement, 75

C
capitalization of earnings, 13
certified appraiser, 7, 62–63
closing the sale, 137–146
    pre-closing checklist, 138–139
collateral, 112, 117
comparable data, 7–8
comparable-sales valuation, 7–8, 75
confidentiality agreement, 63, 75, 78, 93
covenant not to compete, 151

D
digital toolkit, vii
discounted cash flow (DCF), 13
due diligence, 6, 122–129, 151
due diligence required documents, 123–124

E
earnings multiple, 9–11, 17, 75, 117

EBIDTA, 9
entity sale, 51–52, 53
ESOP, 29, 32
exit planning, 22–27, 31
exit strategy, 34–36

F
financial records and documentation, 64–66
franchise resale, 94

G
GAAP, 75
going concern value, 18
goodwill, 18

I
income valuation approach, 4, 12–13, 18
intellectual property, 18
International Business Brokers Association (IBBA), 16
intramarket transaction, 94
IRS asset classes, 133–134

L
legal documentation, 67
letter of intent, 79, 101, 114–115, 117, 151
liquidation, 18, 30

M
maintaining confidentiality, 78–79
marketing your business, 77–90
market valuation approach, 4, 7–9
mergers and acquisitions (M&A), 17, 61

N
negotiating final terms, 137–142
non-disclosure agreement (NDA), 117, 151

O
offer-to-purchase agreement, 75
online business-for-sale sites, 94
owner's cash flow, 9

P
payment approaches, 109–111, 135–136
pre-sale business assessment, 41
pre-sale business improvements, 42–52
prescreening buyers, 92–93
price-to-earnings ratios, 8–9

Index

price-to-revenues ratios, 8–9
pricing your business, 68–70
promissory note, 117, 151
purchase and sale agreement, 140–142, 151
purchase price allocation, 132–134, 151
purchase proposal, 114–115
    letter of intent, 79, 101, 114–115, 117, 151
    responding and accepting, 115–116

R
revenue multiples, 9

S
sale options, 27–31
sale payment structure, 152
sale-readiness assessment, 41–42
sale structure, 50–51, 53, 128–131
SBA 7(a) loan, 118
secured promissory note, 117
seller financing, 14, 18, 32, 51–52, 75, 118
    minimizing risk, 111–113
    pros and cons, 110–111
seller-financing note, 76
seller's discretionary earnings (SDE), 9–10, 18, 75, 118
selling memorandum, 71–75, 76, 118
selling memo summary, 73–74, 76, 118

T
transferring business ownership, 147–148

V
valuation, 3–17
    asset approach, 4, 5–7
    income approach, 4, 12–13
    market approach, 4, 7–11
verifying buyer qualifications, 96–97

W
warranties and representations, 94
weighted average cost of capital (WACC), 13
what buyers want, 37–41

BizBuySell Guide to Selling Your Business

Made in the USA
Columbia, SC
25 July 2023